Dan Cederholm

CSS3 FOR
WEB DESIGNERS

Copyright © 2014 by Dan Cederholm
First edition published 2011
All rights reserved

Publisher: Jeffrey Zeldman
Designer: Jason Santa Maria
Executive Director: Katel LeDû
Technical Editor: Rachel Andrew
Copyeditor: Sally Kerrigan
Compositor: Rob Weychert
Ebook Production: India Amos

Editor, first edition: Mandy Brown
Technical Editor, first edition: Ethan Marcotte
Copyeditor, first edition: Krista Stevens
Compositor, first edition: Neil Egan

ISBN 978-1-9375572-0-1

A Book Apart
New York, New York
http://abookapart.com

10 9 8 7 6 5 4 3 2 1

TABLE OF CONTENTS

FOREWORD

WEBSITES ARE NOT the same as pictures of websites. When one person designs in Photoshop and another converts the design to markup and CSS, the coder must make guesses and assumptions about what the designer intended. This interpretive process is never without friction—unless the coder is Dan Cederholm. When Dan codes other people's designs, he gets everything right, including the parts the designer got wrong. For instance, Dan inevitably translates a designer's fixed Photoshop dimensions into code that is flexible, accessible, and bulletproof. (Indeed, Dan coined the phrase "bulletproof web design" while teaching the rest of us how to do it.)

In Dan's case, flexible never means sloppy. The details always matter. That's because Dan is not only a brilliant front-end developer and user advocate, he is also a designer to his core. He dreams design, bleeds design, and even gave the world a new way to share design at dribbble.com. Dan is also a born teacher and funny guy whose deadpan delivery makes Steven Wright look giddy by comparison. Dan speaks all over, helping designers improve their craft, and he not only educates, he *kills*.

And that, my friends, is why we've asked him to be our (and your) guide to CSS3. You couldn't ask for a smarter, more experienced, more design-focused guide or a bigger web standards geek than our man Dan. Enjoy the trip!

—Jeffrey Zeldman

INTRODUCTION

A LOT HAS PROGRESSED since the initial pressing of this little green book. All good things! Many of the CSS3 properties discussed now have wider browser support, which means you can feel even more confident putting them to use. Several new properties have emerged. The economy is looking—wait.

In this second edition, I've brought everything up to present day. I've removed old hacks that are no longer necessary. And I've added a chapter at the end of the book on *micro* layouts. While we wait patiently for a true cross-browser layout system, work carries on. Fortunately, new specifications such as Flexbox and Multi-column Layout are usable today, when applied to smaller components of the overall design. The new chapter explores those options and how they dovetail our existing CSS3 toolbox.

There's never been a better time to dive into CSS3. I hope you enjoy this updated version of what was a very fun book to write, and I look forward to the myriad ways you'll creatively use CSS3. Onward!

1 USING CSS3 TODAY

LOOKING BACK upon the storied history of CSS, we see some important milestones that have shaped our direction as web designers. These watershed techniques, articles, and events helped us create flexible, accessible websites that we could be proud of both visually as well as under the hood.

You could argue that things began to get interesting back in 2001, when Jeffrey Zeldman wrote "To Hell With Bad Browsers" (http://bkaprt.com/css3-2/1/), signaling the dawn of the CSS Age. This manifesto encouraged designers to push forward and use CSS for more than just link colors and fonts, leaving behind older, incapable browsers that choked on CSS1. Yes, *CSS1*.

We spent the next several years discovering and sharing techniques for using CSS to achieve what we wanted for our clients and bosses. It was an exciting time to be experimenting, pushing boundaries, and figuring out complex ways of handling cross-browser rendering issues—all in the name of increased flexibility, improved accessibility, and reduced code.

Somewhere around 2006 or so, the talk about CSS went quiet. Most of the problems we needed to solve had documented solutions. Common browser bugs had multiple workarounds. We created support groups for designers emotionally scarred by inexplicable Internet Explorer bugs. Our hair started to gray. (OK, I'm speaking for myself here.) Most importantly though, the contemporary crop of browsers was relatively stagnant. This period of status quo gave us time to craft reusable approaches and establish best practices, but things got a little, dare I say, *boring* for the CSS aficionado yearning for better tools.

Thankfully things changed. Browsers began iterating and updating more rapidly (well, some of them anyway). Firefox and Safari not only started to gain market share, they also thrived on a quicker development cycle, adding solid standards support alongside more experimental properties. In many cases, the technologies that these forward-thinking browsers chose to implement were then folded back into draft specifications. In other words, periodically it was the browser vendors that pushed the spec along.

BUT DON'T READ THE SPEC

Ask a roomful of web designers, "Who likes reading specs?" and you might get one person to raise their hand. (If you are that person, I commend you and the free time you apparently have.) Although they serve as important *references,* I certainly don't enjoy reading specifications in their entirety, nor do I recommend doing so in order to grasp CSS3 as a whole.

The good news is that CSS3 is actually a series of *modules* that are designed to be implemented separately and independently from each other. This is a very good thing. This segmented approach has enabled portions of the spec to move faster (or slower) than others, and has encouraged browser vendors to implement the pieces that are further along before the entirety of CSS3 is considered finished.

The W3C (http://bkaprt.com/css3-2/2/) explains the module approach:

Rather than attempting to shove dozens of updates into a single monolithic specification, it will be much easier and more efficient to be able to update individual pieces of the specification. Modules will enable CSS to be updated in a more timely and precise fashion, thus allowing for a more flexible and timely evolution of the specification as a whole.

The benefit here for us web designers is that along with experimentation and faster release cycle comes the ability to use many CSS3 properties before waiting until they become Candidate Recommendations, perhaps years from now.

Now, by all means, if you *enjoy* reading specifications, go for it! Naturally there's a lot to be learned in there—but it's far more practical to focus on what's currently implemented and usable *today,* and those are the bits that we'll be talking about in the rest of this chapter. Later, we'll apply those bits in examples throughout the rest of the book.

I've always learned more about web design by dissecting examples in the wild rather than reading white papers, and that's what we'll stress in the pages that follow.

CSS3 IS FOR EVERYONE

I've been hearing this quite a bit from fellow web designers across the globe: "I can't wait to use CSS3...*when it's supported in all browsers.*"

But the truth is large portions of CSS3 are now very well supported in the majority of browsers, and everyone can begin using CSS3 right now. Fortunately you don't have to think differently or make drastic changes to the way you craft websites in order to do so. How can anyone use CSS3 on any project? By carefully choosing the situations where we apply CSS3, focusing squarely on the *experience layer.*

Targeting the experience layer

If we've been doing things right over the past several years, we've been building upon a foundation of web standards (semantic HTML and CSS for layout, type, color, etc.), leaving many of the interaction effects—animation, feedback, and movement—to technologies like Flash and JavaScript. With CSS3 properties being slowly but steadily introduced in forward-thinking browsers, we can start to shift some of that experience layer to our stylesheets.

As an interface designer who leans heavily toward the visual side of design rather than the programmatic side, the more I can do to make a compelling user experience using already-familiar tools like HTML and CSS, the more I do a happy little dance.

CSS3 is for web designers like you and me, and we can start using portions of it *today,* so long as we know *when* and *how* to fold it in.

When to apply CSS3

In terms of a website's visual experience, we could group things into two categories: *critical* and *non-critical* (**TABLE 1.1**).

Areas like branding, usability, and layout are crucial to any website's success, and as such utilizing technology that's not fully supported by the majority of browsers would be a risky venture there.

For example, in the evolving CSS3 spec there are multiple drafts for controlling layout—something we drastically need. We've been bending the `float` property to handle layout for years now. We've figured out how to get by with what we have, but a real page layout engine is absolutely a necessity.

That said, the new layout modules in CSS3 are still being worked out and/or they have support only in the most recent browsers. While CSS3 gives us some new layout options for certain design patterns (which we'll get into later in the book), for something as important as *page* layout, CSS3 likely isn't the perfect tool. Yet.

On the opposite end of the spectrum are non-critical events like interaction (hover, focus, form elements, browser viewport flexibility), and visual enhancements that result from those interactions (along with animation). It's far less crucial to match an identical experience between browsers for events like these, and

CRITICAL	NON-CRITICAL
Branding	Interaction
Usability	Visual Rewards
Accessibility	Feedback
Layout	Movement

TABLE 1.1: A website's visual experience can be grouped into critical and non-critical categories. The latter are where CSS3 can be applied today.

that's why it's a perfect opportunity to apply certain portions of CSS3 here for browsers that support them now.

It's atop these non-critical events where we'll be applying CSS3 throughout the book, keeping the more important characteristics of the page intact for all browsers, regardless of their current CSS3 support.

When we decide to focus on and target these non-critical areas of the visual experience, it becomes incredibly freeing to layer on CSS3 and enrich the interaction of a website without worrying that the core message, layout, and accessibility will be hindered.

CORE CSS3 PROPERTIES THAT ARE USABLE TODAY

So, while we've pinpointed the experience layer as a place we can safely apply CSS3 today, we'll also want to pinpoint which CSS3 properties we can use. That is, which portions of the spec have a reached enough of a browser implementation tipping point to be practical and usable right now.

Large chunks of CSS3 have not yet been implemented in any browser. Things are still being worked out. We can be curious about those chunks that are in flux, but we're better off focusing

PROPERTY	SUPPORTED IN				
border-radius	3+	3+	1+	10.5+	9+
text-shadow	1.1+	2+	3.1+	9.5+	10+
box-shadow	3+	3+	3.5+	10.5+	9+
box-sizing	3+	3+	2+	9.5+	8+
Multiple background images	1.3+	2+	3.6+	10.5+	9+
opacity	1.2+	1+	1.5+	9+	9+
RGBA	3.2+	3+	3+	10+	9+

TABLE 1.2: CSS3 properties and the browsers that support them.

our attention on what actually works, and lucky for us there's a fair amount now that does.

Let's take a quick look at the relatively small set of core CSS3 properties that we'll be using in the examples in the book (below, and TABLE 1.2). I'm merely introducing them here, as we'll be digging much deeper into advanced syntax and real-world usage later.

border-radius

Rounds the corners of an element with a specified radius value. Supported in Safari 3+, Chrome 3+, Firefox 1+, Opera 10.5+, and IE9+. Example:

```
.foo {
   border-radius: 10px;
}
```

text-shadow

A CSS2 property (dropped in 2.1 then reintroduced in CSS3) that adds a shadow to hypertext, with options for the direction, amount of blur, and color of the shadow. Supported in Safari 1.1+, Chrome 2+, Firefox 3.1+, Opera 9.5+, and IE10+. Example:

```
p {
   text-shadow: 1px 1px 2px #999;
}
```

box-shadow

Adds a shadow to an element. Identical syntax to `text-shadow`. Supported in Safari 3+, Chrome 3+, Firefox 3.5+, Opera 10.5+, and IE9+. Example:

```
.foo {
   box-shadow: 1px 1px 2px #999;
}
```

box-sizing

Normally, padding and borders are *added* to an element's width. This gets annoyingly tricky when assigning percentage-based widths. Applying the `border-box` value will reverse that and the element's width will always be what you declare. For instance, a form input with a 100% width, 10px of padding, and a 2px border will be 100% and not 100% + 24px. Supported in Safari 3+, Chrome 3+, Firefox 2+, Opera 9.5+, and IE8+. Example:

```
input[type="text"] {
    width: 100%;
    padding: 10px;
    border: 2px solid #999;
    box-sizing: border-box;
}
```

Multiple background images

CSS3 adds the ability to apply multiple background images on an element (separated with commas), as opposed to just one as defined in CSS2.1. Supported in Safari 1.3+, Chrome 2+, Firefox 3.6+, Opera 10.5+, and IE9+. Example:

```
body {
    background: url(image1.png) no-repeat top left,
    url(image2.png) repeat-x bottom left,
    url(image3.png) repeat-y top right;
}
```

opacity

Defines how opaque an element is. A value of 1 means completely opaque, while a value of 0 means fully transparent. Supported in Safari 1.2+, Chrome 1+, Firefox 1.5+, Opera 9+, and IE9+. Example:

```
.foo {
    opacity: 0.5; /* .foo will be 50% transparent */
}
```

RGBA

Not a CSS property, but rather a new *color model* introduced in CSS3, adding the ability to specify a level of opacity along with an RGB color value. Supported in Safari 3.2+, Chrome 3+, Firefox 3+, Opera 10+, and IE9+. Example:

```
.foo {
    color: rgba(0, 0, 0, 0.75); /* black at 75% opacity */
}
```

Now that list is far from exhaustive, of course. CSS3 contains many more properties and tools, many of which are still being developed and are not yet implemented in any browser. But you'll notice that each property in the previous list has a reached a certain threshold of browser support: it works in most of the major browsers.

So we now have a nice concise list of properties to play with, based on their relatively decent support in Safari, Chrome, Firefox, Internet Explorer, and Opera. They don't work in older versions of those browsers, but we'll be discussing why that's OK, and how to plan for that non-uniform support later in the book.

What we aren't going to cover

I've listed the handful of CSS3 properties that we'll be using often in the book, but what about the rest? I've chosen not to exhaustively cover everything here, but rather what's practically usable right now because it has decent, stable browser support.

There are also other portions of the CSS3 spec that might be usable today, but are out of the scope of this book (and might warrant a book entirely on their own):

1. Media Queries (http://www.w3.org/TR/CSS3-mediaqueries/)
2. Grid Layout (http://www.w3.org/TR/css3-grid-layout/)
3. CSS3 Selectors (http://www.w3.org/TR/css3-selectors/)
4. Regions (http://www.w3.org/TR/css3-regions/)
5. Web Fonts (http://www.w3.org/TR/CSS3-webfonts/)

Be sure to check out these other modules after you've finished reading this book.

VENDOR-SPECIFIC PREFIXES

I mentioned earlier that the CSS3 specification is a series of modules that are being gradually rolled out by browser vendors. In some cases this rolling out involves experimental support. That is, while the spec is being written, debated, and hashed out at the W3C, a browser maker might choose to add support for certain properties anyway, testing it in a real-world environment. It's become a healthy part of the process, where feedback from experimental usage is often used to make adjustments to the spec.

Alternatively, a browser vendor might want to introduce an experimental property that's not part of any proposed standard, but may become one at a later date.

Often this experimental support for CSS properties is handled by the use of a *vendor prefix* like so:

```
-webkit-border-radius
```

This dash-prefixed keyword attached to the beginning of the property name flags it as a work-in-progress, specific to the browser's implementation and interpretation of the evolving spec. If and when the experiment becomes part of a finished CSS3 module, the browser should support the non-prefixed property name going forward.

Each browser vendor has their own prefix, essentially namespacing their experimental properties. Other browsers will ignore rules containing prefixes they don't recognize.

TABLE 1.3 shows the most widely used vendors and their associated prefixes, and we'll be using the WebKit, Mozilla, and Opera prefixes as they pertain to CSS3 in the examples in the chapters ahead.

How vendor prefixes work

Here's how vendor-prefixed CSS works in practice; we'll use the `border-radius` property as an example. Say we wanted to round the corners of an element with a radius of 10 pixels; here's how we'd do it:

Apple	-webkit-
Google	-webkit-
Mozilla	-moz-
Opera	-o-
Konqueror	-khtml-
Microsoft	-ms-

TABLE 1.3: The most widely-used vendors and their associated prefixes.

```
.foo {
  -webkit-border-radius: 10px;
  -moz-border-radius: 10px;
  border-radius: 10px;
}
```

Earlier versions of WebKit (the engine behind Safari, mobile Safari, and Chrome) and Gecko (the engine behind Firefox) browsers each supported the border-radius property by way of their own vendor-prefixed versions, while Opera 10.5 and IE9+ have supported the property without a vendor prefix.

Optimal ordering

When using vendor prefixes, it's important to keep in mind the order in which you list rules in your declarations. You'll notice in the above example that we listed the vendor-prefixed property first, followed by the non-prefixed CSS3 property.

Why put the actual CSS3 property last? Because your styles will likely work in more browsers in the future, progressively enhancing your designs going forward. And when a browser finally implements support for the property as defined in the specification, that real property will trump the experimental version since it comes last in the list. Should the implementation for the vendor-specific version differ from the real property, you're ensuring that the final standard reigns supreme.

For example, Webkit and Firefox have been supporting non-prefixed border-radius for several versions now. It may be safe to simply use the non-prefixed property, depending on your project. However, there's no harm in continuing to include the vendor prefixes for older browsers.

Don't be afraid of vendor prefixes!

Your initial reaction might be one of, "Blech, this is messy, proprietary stuff!" But I assure you, not only is it a way forward, it's much less messy than the code bloat and inflexibility that often come along with *non*-CSS3 solutions, and an important part of the evolution of the specification as well.

By using these properties now via vendor prefixes, we can test the waters, even giving valuable feedback to browser makers before the spec is final. Remember, too, that the prefixes are usually attached to *proposed standards*. That's a big difference from other hackish CSS we've all periodically used to solve cross-browser issues.

Some might compare vendor prefixes to the syntax exploits many of us have used to target specific browser versions (for example, using w\idth: 200px or _width: 200px to target specific versions of IE). But rather, vendor prefixes are *an important part of the standards process,* allowing the evolution of a property in a real-world implementation.

As CSS expert Eric Meyer explains in "Prefix or Posthack" on A List Apart (http://bkaprt.com/css3-2/3/):

> *Prefixes give us control of our hacking destiny. In the past, we had to invent a bunch of parser exploits just to get inconsistent implementations to act the same once we found out they were*

*inconsistent. It was a wholly reactive approach. Prefixes are a
proactive approach.*

He goes on to suggest that vendor prefixing is not only positive, but should be made more central to the standards process,
and would:

> *...force the vendors and the Working Group to work together to
> devise the tests necessary to determine interoperability. Those
> tests can then guide those who follow, helping them to achieve
> interoperable status much faster. They could literally ship the
> prefixed implementation in one public beta and drop the prefix
> in the next.*

So, don't fret over vendor prefixes. Use them knowing you're
a part of a process that allows you to get work done today, and
paves the way toward a future when prefixes can be dropped.

It's also worth mentioning that Chrome, Mozilla, and even
the W3C are headed toward ditching the concept of vendor prefixes altogether (http://bkaprt.com/css3-2/4/). For now, they're
necessary, but the future could very well be vendor-prefix-less,
where experimental features would be hidden behind special
browser preferences. That'll make using in-progress properties
a bit harder for us to implement before full support is offered,
which is a bit of a bummer. Something to keep an eye on!

What about all that repetition?

You might think it's silly to have to repeat what seems like the
same property three or four times for each vendor, and I might
agree with you.

But the reality is that non-CSS3 solutions would likely require
inflexible and more complex code, albeit perhaps non-repetitive.

We won't need to repeat ourselves forever. For now, it's
a necessary but temporary step to keep potentially varying
implementations between browsers separate from the final spec
implementation. Fortunately, CSS preprocessors like Sass and
LESS help immensely in regards to writing vendor prefix patterns once, keeping them quarantined and easily updated for an

entire project. For more on getting started with Sass, check out my *Sass for Web Designers* book, also from A Book Apart.

Before we start doing compelling things with the handful of usable CSS3 properties and their respective vendor prefixes, let's get a basic grasp on CSS transitions. Understanding transitions and how they operate will help us combine them with other properties to create wonderful experiences.

2 UNDERSTANDING CSS TRANSITIONS

IT WAS 1997 and I was sitting in a terribly run-down apartment in beautiful Allston, Massachusetts. A typical late night of viewing source and teaching myself HTML followed a day of packing CDs at a local record label for peanuts (hence the run-down apartment). I'm sure you can relate.

One triumphant night, I pumped my fist in sweet victory. I'd just successfully coded my first JavaScript image rollover. Remember those?

I still remember the amazement of seeing a crudely designed button graphic I'd cobbled together "swap" to a different one when hovered over by the mouse. I barely had a clue as to what I was doing at the time, but making something on the page successfully change, *dynamically,* was, well…magical.

We've come a *long* way over the past decade in regard to interaction and visual experience on the web. Historically, technologies like Flash and JavaScript have enabled animation, movement, and interaction effects. But recently, with browsers rolling out support for CSS transitions and transforms, some of that animation and experience enrichment can now be comfortably moved to our stylesheets.

My first JavaScript rollover back in 1997 took me several nights of head scratching, many lines of code that seemed alien to me at the time, and multiple images. CSS3 today enables far richer, more flexible interactions through simple lines of code that thankfully degrade gracefully in the browsers that don't yet support it.

As I mentioned in Chapter 1, we can start to use some CSS3 properties right now as long as we carefully choose the situations in which to use them. The same could be said for CSS transitions. They certainly won't *replace* existing technologies like Flash, JavaScript, or SVG (especially without broader browser support)—but in conjunction with the aforementioned core CSS3 properties (and CSS transforms and animations which we'll cover later in the book), they can be used to push the experience layer a notch higher. And most importantly, they're relatively easy to implement for the web designer already familiar with CSS. It only takes a few lines of code.

I'm introducing CSS transitions early here in Chapter 2, as we'll be applying them to many of the examples later in the book. Having a basic understanding of the syntax of transitions and how they work will be beneficial before we dig deeper into a case study.

TAIL WAGGING THE DOG

Initially developed solely by the WebKit team for Safari, CSS Transitions are now a Working Draft specification at the W3C. (CSS Transforms and CSS Animations share that same lineage, and we'll be talking about them in Chapters 4 and 6, respectively.)

This is a nice example of browser innovation being folded back into a potential standard. I say *potential* since it's still a Working Draft today (meaning the spec is still in flux and could change before becoming finalized). However, CSS transition support can be found in Safari 3+, Chrome 2+, Firefox 4+, Opera 10.5+, and IE10+. In other words, while it is a *draft* specification and evolving, it has plenty of solid support and has come a long way from its humble beginnings as a proprietary Safari-only experiment.

Let's take a look at how transitions work, shall we? Like the CSS3 properties discussed in Chapter 1, I'm only introducing them here along with their basic syntax so you'll have a good handle on how they operate. Later, we'll be doing all sorts of fun things with transitions, using them to polish the examples in the chapters ahead, and you'll be up to speed on how transitions properly fit into the mix.

WHAT ARE CSS TRANSITIONS?

I like to think of CSS transitions like *butter*, smoothing out value changes in your stylesheets when triggered by interactions like hovering, clicking, and focusing. Unlike real butter, transitions aren't fattening—they're just a few simple rules in your stylesheet to enrich certain events in your designs.

The W3C explains CSS transitions quite simply (http://bkaprt. com/css3-2/5/):

CSS Transitions allow property changes in CSS values to occur smoothly over a specified duration.

This smoothing animates the changing of a CSS value when triggered by a mouse click, focus or active state, or any changes to the element (including even a change on the element's class attribute).

A SIMPLE EXAMPLE

Let's start with a simple example, where we'll add a transition to the background color swap of a link. When hovered over, the link's background color will change, and we'll use a transition

FIG 2.1: The normal and :hover state of the link.

FIG 2.2: The printed page sure is a clunky way to display an animated transition, but this figure attempts to do just that, showing the smooth transition of light green to darker green background.

to smooth out that change—an effect previously only possible using Flash or JavaScript, but now possible with a few simple lines of CSS.

The markup is a simple hyperlink, like so:

```
<a href="#" class="foo">Transition me!</a>
```

Next, we'll add a declaration for the normal link state with a little padding and a light green background, followed by the background swap to a darker green on hover (**FIG 2.1**):

```
a.foo {
    padding: 5px 10px;
    background: #9c3;
}

a.foo:hover {
    background: #690;
}
```

Now let's add a transition to that background color change. This will smooth out and animate the difference over a specified period of time (**FIG 2.2**).

For the time being, we'll use only the non-vendor-prefixed properties to keep things simple. Later, we'll add vendor prefixes for older versions of WebKit, Mozilla, and Opera.

```
a.foo {
  padding: 5px 10px;
  background: #9c3;
  transition-property: background;
  transition-duration: 0.3s;
  transition-timing-function: ease;
}

a.foo:hover {
  background: #690;
}
```

You'll notice the three parts of a transition in the declaration:

- transition-property: The property to be transitioned (in this case, the background property)
- transition-duration: How long the transition should last (0.3 seconds)
- transition-timing-function: How fast the transition happens over time (ease)

TIMING FUNCTIONS (OR, I REALLY WISH I'D PAID ATTENTION IN MATH CLASS)

The timing function value allows the speed of the transition to change over time by defining one of six possibilities: ease, linear, ease-in, ease-out, ease-in-out, and cubic-bezier (which allows you to define your own timing curve).

If you slept through geometry in high school like I did, don't worry. I recommend simply plugging in each of these timing function values to see how they differ.

For our simple example, the duration of the transition is so quick (just a mere 0.3 seconds) that it'd be difficult to tell the difference between the six options. For longer animations, the timing function you choose becomes a more important piece of the puzzle, as there's time to notice the speed changes over the length of the animation.

When in doubt, `ease` (which is also the default value) or `linear` should work just fine for short transitions.

DELAYING THE TRANSITION

Going back to our example, transitions can be delayed from the moment the trigger happens on screen. For example, let's say we wanted the background transition to happen half a second *after* the link is hovered over. We can do that using the `transition-delay` property.

```
a.foo {
    padding: 5px 10px;
    background: #9c3;
    transition-property: background;
    transition-duration: 0.3s;
    transition-timing-function: ease;
    transition-delay: 0.5s;
}

a.foo:hover {
    background: #690;
}
```

SHORTHAND TRANSITIONS

We could simplify the (non-delayed) declaration significantly by using the transition shorthand property, which is the syntax we'll be using in the examples later in the book.

```
a.foo {
    padding: 5px 10px;
    background: #9c3;
    transition: background 0.3s ease;
}
```

```
a.foo:hover {
  background: #690;
}
```

Now we have a much more compact rule that accomplishes the same result.

Shorthand transition with a delay

If we wanted to add back in the half-second delay to the shorthand version of the transition, we can do that by placing the duration value at the end of the rule, like this:

```
a.foo {
  padding: 5px 10px;
  background: #9c3;
  transition: background 0.3s ease 0.5s;
}

a.foo:hover {
  background: #690;
}
```

Now sure, all of this wonderful transitioning looks rather simple and fun, but what about browser support?

BROWSER SUPPORT

As I mentioned earlier, transitions were initially developed by WebKit, and have been in Safari and Chrome since version 3.2, but Opera supports them as well from version 10.5 onward (http://bkaprt.com/css3-2/6/), Firefox 4.0 and above (http://bkaprt.com/css3-2/7/), and Internet Explorer 10+.

WebKit, Mozilla, and Opera initially supported transitions by way of vendor prefixing, and while current versions of those browsers no longer require vendor prefixes, it can't hurt adding them in for visitors using older versions. Note that Internet Explorer has only supported transitions *without* a vendor prefix starting with version 10.

BUILDING THE FULL TRANSITION STACK

Here's a revised declaration, adding the `-moz-` and `-o-` prefixes as well as the actual CSS3 `transition` property. Again, we're putting the non-prefixed property *last* in the stack to ensure that the final implementation will trump the others as the property moves from draft to finished status or as the browser manufacturer decides to remove the prefix.

```
a.foo {
  padding: 5px 10px;
  background: #9c3;
  -webkit-transition: background 0.3s ease;
  -moz-transition: background 0.3s ease;
  -o-transition: background 0.3s ease;
  transition: background 0.3s ease;
}

a.foo:hover {
  background: #690;
}
```

With that stack, we'll be smoothing out that background color change in current versions of Safari, Chrome, Internet Explorer, and Opera, as well as future versions of any browser that chooses to support it.

TRANSITIONING STATES

I remember being slightly confused when I first started playing around with CSS Transitions. Wouldn't it make more sense if the transition properties were placed in the :hover declaration, since that's the trigger for the transition? The answer is that there are other possible states of an element besides :hover, and you'll likely want that transition to happen on each of those without duplication.

For instance, you may want the transition to happen on the :focus or :active pseudo-classes of the link as well. Instead of having to add the transition property stack to each of those declarations, the transition instructions are attached to the normal state and therefore declared only once.

The following example adds the same background switch to the :focus state. This enables triggering the transition from either hovering over *or* focusing the link (via the keyboard, for example).

```
a.foo {
    padding: 5px 10px;
    background: #9c3;
    -webkit-transition: background 0.3s ease;
    -moz-transition: background 0.3s ease;
    -o-transition: background 0.3s ease;
    transition: background 0.3s ease;
}

a.foo:hover,
a.foo:focus {
    background: #690;
}
```

TRANSITIONING MULTIPLE PROPERTIES

Let's say that along with the background color, we also want to change the link's text color and transition that as well. We can do that by stringing multiple transitions together, separated by a comma. Each can have varying duration and timing functions (**FIG 2.3**). *(Line wraps marked ».)*

```
a.foo {
  padding: 5px 10px;
  background: #9c3;
  -webkit-transition: background .3s ease, »
    color 0.2s linear;
  -moz-transition: background .3s ease, »
    color 0.2s linear;
  -o-transition: background .3s ease, color 0.2s linear;
  transition: background .3s ease, color 0.2s linear;
}

a.foo:hover,
a.foo:focus {
  color: #030;
  background: #690;
}
```

TRANSITIONING ALL POSSIBLE PROPERTIES

An alternative to listing multiple properties is using the `all` value. This will transition all available properties.

Let's drop `all` into our simple example instead of listing `background` and `color` separately. They'll now share the same duration and timing function.

```
a.foo {
  padding: 5px 10px;
  background: #9c3;
  -webkit-transition: all 0.3s ease;
  -moz-transition: all 0.3s ease;
  -o-transition: all 0.3s ease;
  transition: all  0.3s ease;
}

a.foo:hover,
a.foo:focus {
  color: #030;
  background: #690;
}
```

This is a convenient way of catching all the changes that happen on :hover, :focus, or :active events without having to list each property you'd like to transition.

WHICH CSS PROPERTIES CAN BE TRANSITIONED?

Now that we've successfully transitioned the background and color of a hyperlink, there are many other CSS properties that can be transitioned, including width, opacity, position, and font-size. A chart of all the possible properties (and their types) that can be transitioned is available from the W3C (http://bkaprt. com/css3-2/8/).

The opportunities for wonderfully fluid experiences are clear. We'll be using several of these properties in conjunction with transitions throughout our case study examples in the next chapter and onward.

WHY NOT USE JAVASCRIPT INSTEAD?

You might be wondering, with not all browsers supporting (or at least promising support for) CSS Transitions, why not use a JavaScript solution to handle the animation? Popular frameworks such as jQuery, Prototype, and script.aculo.us have enabled animations via JavaScript that work cross-browser for some time now.

It all depends on how crucial the transitions are to the experience. I'm stressing here in this little book that you can embrace the simplicity and flexibility of CSS3 if you choose the appropriate parts of the user experience to apply it: enriching the interactions that happen on the page. Quite often, the animation of these interactions when handled by CSS Transitions aren't integral to the brand, readability, or layout of the website.

Therefore, a few simple lines of CSS to trigger a simple animation that's *native* to the browsers that support it (rather than tapping into a JavaScript framework) seems like a smart choice. And one I'm glad we have at our disposal.

BE SMART, BE SUBTLE

Like all shiny new tools, it's important to use transitions *appropriately*. One can easily go overboard adding transitions to everything on the page, resulting in some sort of annoying, pulsating monster. It's key to decide where transitions rightfully enrich the user experience and when they are just extraneous noise. Additionally, making sure the speed of the transition doesn't slow down an otherwise snappy action from the user is crucial. Use with care and caution.

For more thoughts on appropriate speeds for CSS transitions and animations, see Trent Walton's post on the subject: http://bkaprt.com/css3-2/9/.

Now that we have a solid base knowledge of how CSS transitions work at a technical level, we can use them to smooth out the experience layer in the examples that follow, beginning with the very next chapter. Let's get to it.

3 HOVER-CRAFTING WITH CSS3

WE'VE SPENT the first two chapters in training, getting up to speed with what's currently usable today in terms of CSS3. We also talked about how the *experience layer* is currently the most appropriate place to apply that usable CSS3.

To recap the important bits we've covered so far, let's keep in mind that:

1. There are core CSS3 properties that are usable today.
2. Everyone can use these core properties in their own projects, especially when targeted at the experience layer.
3. Vendor prefixes allow us to push forward right now, helping test in-flux properties in real-world contexts.
4. CSS Transitions are no longer proprietary experiments, but draft specifications that other browsers are embracing. Let's use 'em!

With all of this under our anti-gravity belts, it's now time to have fun with all our new tools, and put them to work in the context of a full-page design.

FIG 3.1: Our fictional case study, *Things We Left on the Moon.*

OUR CASE STUDY

For most of the following examples I'll be using a fictional case study I've designed: a humorous homage to all the things left on the moon by the astronauts lucky enough to have traveled there (**FIG 3.1**). There's a story behind the subject matter that directly relates to the theme of this book, if you'll bear with me for just a bit.

Messages in space and on the web

In 1969, astronauts Neil Armstrong and Buzz Aldrin became the first humans to set foot on the moon. I've been a casual fan of space travel and the NASA program, but hearing more about the Apollo 11 mission around the fortieth anniversary inspired me to read more about the history and events surrounding the

FIG 3.2: The small (about the size of a U.S. half-dollar) silicon disc left on the moon by the Apollo 11 astronauts. (NASA/courtesy of nasaimages.org)

landing. In particular, I was fascinated by all the stuff that was left on the moon and remains up there to this day.

Out of all the objects that have been left behind, there's one in particular that I found extremely interesting, and it serves as a wonderful example of user experience design. It's a small, silicon disc (about the size of a US half dollar). Etched on the disc are goodwill messages from the leaders of over seventy countries from around the world. You need a microscope to read them, but limitations in regard to what the astronauts could bring with them helped shape the design of a commemorative object that could be left on the moon for future visitors to discover (**FIG 3.2**).

NASA was, in a sense, designing an object using the latest technology available at the time, for an unknown audience sometime in the future. Sound familiar?

Later, in 1977, a similar design problem was solved for the Voyager 1 and Voyager 2 spacecraft by way of the Golden Record: a gold-plated copper phonograph record that contains

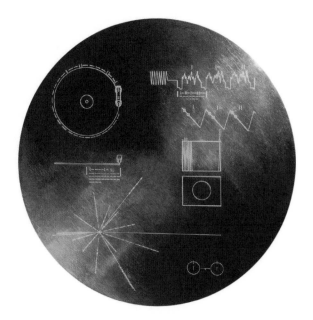

FIG 3.3: The gold-plated outer case of the Golden Record, a phonograph record aboard the Voyager 1 and 2 spacecraft. (Courtesy NASA/JPL-Caltech)

audio, images, and diagrams from life here on Earth (**FIG 3.3**). In a sense the record is a message in a bottle to potential civilizations beyond our solar system. On its case is etched symbolic language, depicting how to properly play the record, where in the galaxy it came from, and other instructions.

Like the silicon disc still resting in moon dust, the Golden Record was designed using the latest technology on hand at the time it was made, for a user experience with numerous unknowns. Would the alien retrievers of the record be able to see, feel, and listen to its contents?

We can learn a lot from the silicon disc left on the moon and the Golden Record hurtling into deep space—that utilizing the best technology possible can help support the message being sent to a largely unknown audience.

As web designers, we too are sending messages in a bottle when we create things for the web. We can make assumptions about who will be reading them, what they're actually capable of understanding, etc.—but we're never 100% informed. That shouldn't prevent us from using the best technology available to deliver that message and the experience around it, letting the experience degrade gracefully in older or less capable devices. Our job as designers is not to simply dress up the bottle and make it look pretty, but rather to find ways to enrich the story and enhance the message. CSS3 can help us do that today.

So now you know why our case study pays homage to those messages left on the moon or floating through space. It's time to start dissecting the site, breaking it into bite-sized examples as they pertain to CSS3. I find it helpful to collect all the techniques we'll be discussing in a single place. You'll be able to reference this template and all the examples whenever you'd like in a living, breathing, one-page website.

You can download the case study's example code at http://CSS3exp.com/code.

Each of the remaining chapters tackles a different set of examples related to CSS3. Instead of attempting to be all-inclusive, telling you everything there is to know about CSS3, I'm doing quite the opposite here: diving into very specific, targeted examples, while showing how they work in a simulated context—quick takeaways that you'll be able to apply immediately and build upon after digesting these pages. *Burp.*

SURPRISE AND DELIGHT

Part of what makes designing for the web so different and interesting as opposed to static media is *interaction.* Things can react, move, and even surprise when experienced in pixels rather than paper.

And it's the interaction that's so easily enhanced by CSS3 for browsers that support it, yet not missed by those that don't.

A wonderful example of surprising and delighting with CSS3 can be found on Dutch designer and developer Faruk Ateş's personal site (http://farukat.es). In the sidebar is a list of links to various social networks that, on hover, expand and come alive with several CSS3 treatments and a smooth transition (**FIG 3.4**).

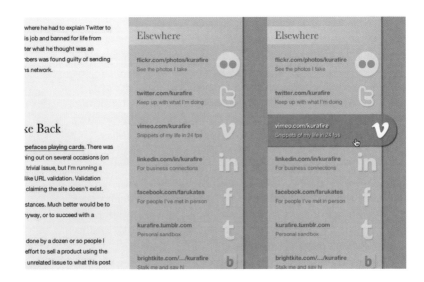

where he had to explain Twitter to is job and banned for life from ter what he thought was an ıbers was found guilty of sending ıs network.

Elsewhere

flickr.com/photos/kurafire
See the photos I take

twitter.com/kurafire
Keep up with what I'm doing

vimeo.com/kurafire
Snippets of my life in 24 fps

linkedin.com/in/kurafire
For business connections

facebook.com/farukates
For people I've met in person

kurafire.tumblr.com
Personal sandbox

brightkite.com/.../kurafire
Stalk me and say hi

Elsewhere

flickr.com/photos/kurafire
See the photos I take

twitter.com/kurafire
Keep up with what I'm doing

vimeo.com/kurafire
Snippets of my life in 24 fps

linkedin.com/in/kurafire
For business connections

facebook.com/farukates
For people I've met in person

kurafire.tumblr.com
Personal sandbox

brightkite.com/.../kurafire
Stalk me and say hi

‹e Back

pefaces playing cards. There was ıing out on several occasions (on trivial issue, but I'm running a like URL validation. Validation claiming the site doesn't exist.

stances. Much better would be to ıyway, or to succeed with a

done by a dozen or so people I effort to sell a product using the unrelated issue to what this post

FIG 3.4: The sidebar and hover treatment found on Faruk Ateş's site.

What looks like a normal list of text with images floated off to the right turns into something far more interesting when you interact with it. This is a prime example of enriching the experience layer, and Faruk uses a variety of CSS3 properties in order to make that happen (in the browsers that support them). **FIGURE 3.5** shows the same default and hover state as viewed in Internet Explorer 7, which doesn't support CSS3 at all. But you'll notice that, while the hover state isn't as polished, it's still a usable, readable, and *functional* experience—not to mention the default, non-hovered state is nearly identical.

Hovering over (or focusing on) an element is a wonderful place to enhance things with CSS3. Users of Internet Explorer will get a different experience (until it eventually folds in support for CSS3 properties). But this alternate experience is perfectly fine, not unexpected, and frankly IE users won't know what they're missing.

That is, until they fire this up in their friend's copy of Safari, Chrome, Firefox, or Opera (and feel a flush of jealousy).

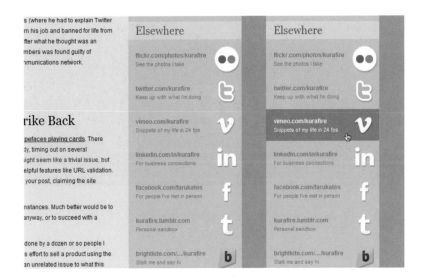

FIG 3.5: Viewed in IE7, Faruk Ateş's site doesn't feature the same visual treatment via CSS3, but that's perfectly OK.

DO WEBSITES NEED TO BE EXPERIENCED EXACTLY THE SAME IN EVERY BROWSER?

It's an important question (and an appropriate one to ask at this point), and I attempt to answer it on this enormously long domain (**FIG 3.6**): http://dowebsitesneedtobeexperiencedexactly thesameineverybrowser.com.

Like Faruk's example, it's not until you start to interact with the site that things get interesting. On the surface, the site looks nearly identical in most browsers, but the moment you move the mouse across the screen and text (**FIG 3.7**), a series of CSS3 properties, transitions, and transforms are applied to make the experience a unique and memorable one.

Once again, it's within the experience layer that we're progressively enriching this web design. The core content, readability, usability, and markup remain consistent and uncompromised.

FIG 3.6: The curiously named http://dowebsitesneedtobeexperiencedexactly thesameineverybrowser.com.

FIG 3.7: An enriched experience is revealed when the site is interacted with. Made possible by our friend CSS3.

NAVIGATING THE MOON

Let's take the concept of adding CSS3 to the hover interactions of a design right to our case study. I'll walk us through the creation of the top navigation of the site (FIG 3.8), where we combine `border-radius`, `text-shadow`, RGBA, and CSS transitions to create an experience that surprises and delights.

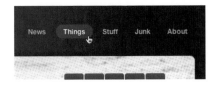

FIG 3.8: The top navigation of our case study, enriched with CSS3 when hovered.

First, the markup

Being good semanticians, we'll markup the top navigation with a good ol' unordered list.

```
<ul id="nav">
  <li><a href="#">News</a></li>
  <li><a href="#">Things</a></li>
  <li><a href="#">Stuff</a></li>
  <li><a href="#">Junk</a></li>
  <li><a href="#">About</a></li>
</ul>
```

Nothing earth-shattering here of course—just an appropriate structure we can use to start applying styles.

Floating the items

First, let's float the entire list and use a bit of padding to position it over to the right of the page; then, let's also float each list item.

```
#nav {
  float: right;
  padding: 42px 0 0 30px;
}

#nav li {
  float: left;
  margin: 0 0 0 5px;
}
```

FIGURE 3.9 shows the result. Our list is now horizontal.

FIG 3.9: A list of links, turned horizontal by a few CSS rules.

FIG 3.10: Links now styled with RGBA, blending the text into the background a bit.

FIG 3.11: A zoomed-in view of the semi-transparent links.

Styling the link color with RGBA

Next, let's add some padding to each link, and change the color to a semi-transparent white. We'll use RGBA to assign white (255, 255, 255) at 70% opacity (0.7), letting the text soak up some of the background color behind it (**FIG 3.10**).

```
#nav li a {
    padding: 5px 15px;
    font-weight: bold;
    color: rgba(255, 255, 255, 0.7);
    }
```

FIGURE 3.11 shows a close up of the links, where the white at 70% opacity via RGBA lets the background shine through, ever so slightly.

Providing a backup for RGBA

RGBA is an amazingly flexible way of specifying color along with a level of opacity, and it has support in recent flavors of Safari, Chrome, Firefox, Opera, and IE9+. But what about older browsers?

Here's where specifying a *backup* color comes into play. When using RGBA to assign color values, it's good practice to specify a solid color first, as a fallback for older browsers that don't support RGBA.

```
#nav li a {
    padding: 5px 15px;
    font-weight: bold;
    color: #ccc;
    color: rgba(255, 255, 255, 0.7);
}
```

Browsers that *do* support RGBA will override the solid color (a light gray #ccc in this case), while browsers that *don't* yet support RGBA yet will ignore the RGBA rule.

So, an important point to remember: specify solid backups for RGBA colors in a separate rule that appears before the RGBA rule.

Adding text-shadow

For one last addition to the link styling, let's add a very subtle text-shadow. We'll use RGBA again here to define the shadow's color, letting the semi-transparent black at 50% opacity blend into the background behind it.

```
#nav li a {
    padding: 5px 15px;
    font-weight: bold;
    color: #ccc;
    color: rgba(255, 255, 255, 0.7);
    text-shadow: 0 1px 1px rgba(0, 0, 0, 0.5);
}
```

FIG 3.12: Comparison of links without text-shadow applied (left) and with text-shadow applied (right).

FIGURE 3.12 shows a comparison of the text links without text-shadow applied (left) and with text-shadow applied (right), as viewed in Safari. It's an almost imperceptible detail, yet the tiny shadow gives the text just enough "lift" off the space background behind it.

Remember that text-shadow works in recent versions of Safari, Chrome, Firefox, Opera, and IE. Browsers that don't support text-shadow will harmlessly ignore the rule. No shadow, no problem.

With the text-shadow in place, we're now free to move on to the :hover treatment. And here's where we'll lean more heavily on CSS3.

Hover and focus styles

We're going to add a color change and background color to the :hover state of each link. Once again, we'll use RGBA to set a semi-transparent white background behind the text on :hover.

```
#nav li a {
    padding: 5px 15px;
    font-weight: bold;
    color: #ccc;
    color: rgba(255, 255, 255, 0.7);
    text-shadow: 0 1px 1px rgba(0, 0, 0, 0.5);
}

#nav li a:hover,
#nav li a:focus {
    color: #fff;
    background: rgba(255, 255, 255, 0.15);
}
```

So, on :hover, we're changing the text color to solid white, and adding a background color of white at 15% opacity. I've also gone ahead and declared this style for when links are *focused* as well. Users navigating with the keyboard, for instance, will then see this change when each link is focused.

FIGURE 3.13 shows the new :hover (and :focus) state of the links. Browsers that support RGBA will get the semi-transparent white background behind brighter white text.

Rounding the hover with border-radius

Going a step further, we could round the corners of the hover background using the CSS3 border-radius property, creating a pill shape for browsers that support it. Specifying 50% here will ensure perfectly round ends, regardless of the font size.

Remembering what we learned back in Chapter 1 about the border-radius property and the vendor prefixes that enable us to use it today, we can add our stack to the default link declaration like so:

```
#nav li a {
  padding: 5px 15px;
  font-weight: bold;
  color: #ccc;
  color: rgba(255, 255, 255, 0.7);
  text-shadow: 0 1px 1px rgba(0, 0, 0, 0.5);
  -webkit-border-radius: 50%;
  -moz-border-radius: 50%;
  border-radius: 50%;
}
```

```
#nav li a:hover,
#nav li a:focus {
  color: #fff;
  background: rgba(255, 255, 255, 0.15);
}
```

FIGURE 3.14 shows the :hover background treatment now with rounded corners via border-radius, which will be seen in Safari, Chrome, Firefox, and Opera, as well as IE9. And remember, we've placed the non-prefixed border-radius property *last* in the list, ensuring the ultimate implementation will trump the vendor-prefixed ones. For example, from version 5, Safari supports both the *non*-prefixed border-radius property as well as -webkit-border-radius.

You might be wondering why I'm placing the border-radius rules in the #nav li a declaration and not in the #nav li a:hover declaration (where it's being revealed). The answer lies in the CSS transition we're going to add next as a final bit of polish.

Adding a transition

Lastly, let's take what we learned in Chapter 2 and add a transition to the :hover and :focus on the nav links. This will smooth out the appearance of the background pill, subtly bringing it into focus behind the text. The transition will also smooth out the text color change from semi-transparent white to fully white (**FIG 3.15**).

Here, we'll add the stack for transitions that currently work in recent versions of the major browsers, with the non-prefixed transition property last in the declaration for eventual implementation by additional browsers (or future versions).

FIG 3.15: Imagine, if you will, the easing in and out when the transition is in place.

```
#nav li a {
  padding: 5px 15px;
  font-weight: bold;
  color: #ccc;
  color: rgba(255, 255, 255, 0.7);
  text-shadow: 0 1px 1px rgba(0, 0, 0, 0.5);
  -webkit-border-radius: 50%;
  -moz-border-radius: 50%;
  border-radius: 50%;
  -webkit-transition: all 0.3s ease-in-out;
  -moz-transition: all 0.3s ease-in-out;
  -o-transition: all 0.3s ease-in-out;
  transition: all 0.3s ease-in-out;
}

#nav li a:hover,
#nav li a:focus {
  color: #fff;
  background: rgba(255, 255, 255, 0.15);
}
```

Remember that we add the transition properties to the normal state of the element to be transitioned. Transitions are designed this way in order for the transition to happen not only on :hover, but also on :focus or :active states as well.

I'm using the `all` value in our transition to catch *all* the properties that change on `:hover` and `:focus`—in this case, color and background. Alternatively, we could've achieved the same transition by listing each of those properties explicitly in a comma-delimited list like this:

```
-webkit-transition:
    color 0.3s ease-in-out,
    background 0.3s ease-in-out;
-moz-transition:
    color 0.3s ease-in-out,
    background 0.3s ease-in-out;
-o-transition:
    color 0.3s ease-in-out,
    background 0.3s ease-in-out;
transition:
    color .3s ease-in-out,
    background .3s ease-in-out;
```

You can quickly see how the `all` value is a bit more compact and efficient for transitioning multiple changes on an element.

Hover-crafting the experience

We've just walked through a rather simple example, adding various CSS3 properties to the experience layer. Browsers that are capable will ease in a semi-transparent, rounded background color behind text-shadowed text links. Browsers that aren't capable don't get the enhanced hover experience, but that's perfectly OK. What they do get is a semantically structured horizontal list of links—and that foundation is what's most important here.

I think this little exercise also demonstrates how efficient it is to achieve something that previously would have required Flash and/or JavaScript to achieve. The CSS rules that we used are simple and straightforward, harmless for browsers that don't yet support them.

We've also future-proofed our CSS3 by ensuring that the `transition` property from the spec is included last in our rules.

Duplicating these rules with the appropriate vendor-specific prefixes is a necessary effort, but one where the payoff is golden: getting to use CSS3 *right now* to enhance the experience for many users.

SIMPLE AND FLEXIBLE HOVERING USING OPACITY

We're constantly looking for solutions that save time and offer additional flexibility. This is precisely what CSS3 offers us in spades: the ability to achieve, in a few lines of code, what used to take more time and resources to create and maintain.

Yet another tool for the hover-crafting arsenal is the opacity property. As mentioned in Chapter 1, opacity is a CSS3 property that allows you to specify how opaque a given element is. Coupled with the aforementioned RGBA, opacity offers another method to add transparency to the designs we create for the web.

One of the ways I like to use opacity is to create simple and flexible hover states for hyperlinked graphics, using the variation in transparency to create multiple states from a single image. Add a CSS transition into the mix and you now have a wonderfully rich experience for linked graphics on the page that's easy to maintain.

Let's take a look at how the opacity property is used on the moon case study.

Opacity on clickable images

FIGURE 3.16 shows the footer of the moon example site, where—underneath some legal copy and a shocking disclaimer—sit three clickable logos.

We're going to use the opacity property to not only control the :hover and :focus treatment, but also to set the *initial* level of transparency. And a CSS transition will smooth out and animate that change for a complete effect.

FIG 3.16: The footer of *Things We Left on the Moon.*

FIG 3.17: The logo PNGs are created fully-white.

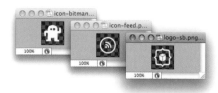

The markup

Like the previous top navigation example, the markup for these footer logos is simple and semantic—just an unordered list of hyperlinked images:

```
<ul id="footer-logos">
  <li><a href="#"><img src="img/logo-sb.png" »
    alt="SimpleBits logo" /></a>
  </li>
  <li><a href="#"><img src="img/icon-feed.png" »
    alt="RSS feed" /></a>
  </li>
  <li><a href="#"><img src="img/icon-bitman.png" »
    alt="BitMan" /></a>
  </li>
</ul>
```

Opacity and image efficiency

I've actually created the icons themselves as fully white PNG images, knowing that I can later use the opacity property to adjust

FIG 3.18: The white PNGs centered in the footer.

the level of transparency with CSS. This has changed the way I think about graphic assets for web projects in some situations.

Instead of saving semi-transparent PNGs, I'll save fully opaque versions (**FIG 3.17**) that I can adjust in the browser. This not only saves time, it also allows us to vary that opacity level on :hover, :focus, and :active states without needing to create multiple sets of images.

Styling the list

The first bits of style will center the images in the footer, and make them horizontal instead of vertical (**FIG 3.18**).

```
#footer-logos {
   text-align: center;
   }

#footer-logos li {
   display: inline;
   }
```

Next, let's add the opacity values that will dim the icons in their default state, brightening them up a bit when hovered or focused.

```
#footer-logos a img {
   opacity: 0.25;
   }
```

```
#footer-logos a:hover img,
#footer-logos a:focus img {
  opacity: 0.6;
}
```

Here we're showing the images at 25% opacity, then bringing them up to 60% opacity when hovered or focused (**FIG 3.19**). Quite a simple thing, isn't it? And it requires only one setof images. Note that the `opacity` property doesn't require vendor prefixes, and will work in Safari, Chrome, Firefox, Opera, and IE9+.

Adding a transition

Lastly, adding a transition to the `opacity` swap will smooth out that value change, and provide a bit of animated richness that'll tie this whole technique together.

Let's add our (now familiar) `transition` stack to the declaration, this time transitioning the `opacity` property specifically. We'll make it rather quick (just 0.2 seconds) and ease it in and then out again.

```
#footer-logos a img {
  opacity: 0.25;
  -webkit-transition: opacity 0.2s ease-in-out;
  -moz-transition: opacity 0.2s ease-in-out;
  -o-transition: opacity 0.2s ease-in-out;
  transition: opacity 0.2s ease-in-out;
}

#footer-logos a:hover img,
#footer-logos a:focus img {
  opacity: 0.6;
}
```

With the transition in place, we now have a simple technique for using opacity to craft a flexible hover experience using a single set of images.

FIG 3.19: Showing the :hover state of the icons in the footer by adjusting the opacity.

GO FORTH AND HOVER-CRAFT

As I mentioned before, this solution has affected the way I think about creating the asset graphics for a design. We can use opacity to control how the graphic appears by default, blending it into the background—then applying a different value for :hover, :focus, and :active states, tying it together with a transition for browsers that support it.

Keep the opacity property in mind next time you're creating hover treatments for hyperlinked images in your own designs. You'll save time, bandwidth, and the unnecessary complexity that other solutions might require.

Hover-crafting with CSS3 is about quickly and efficiently adding simple styles that enrich the experience layer, surprising and delighting users with the browsers that support those properties now and into the future. If the browser doesn't support the high-fidelity experience you've created, that's perfectly OK, as they won't know what they're missing.

4 TRANSFORMING THE MESSAGE

LIKE CSS TRANSITIONS, CSS Transforms were also initially developed by the WebKit team, then folded back into two separate specs at the W3C for 2D and 3D, and ultimately combined into one Working Draft (http://bkaprt.com/css3-2/10/)

We're going to focus primarily on 2D transforms in this book, as they're the most practical to use right now. An entire book could be filled with information on 3D transforms alone, and they're wonderfully magical. But 2D transforms have the most traction with regard to browser support, including Safari 3.2+, Chrome 3.2+, Firefox 4.0+, Opera 10.5+, and IE 9+ (just like transitions).

So just what are CSS Transforms? The W3C (http://bkaprt. com/css3-2/10/) describes them as:

> CSS Transforms allows elements styled with CSS to be transformed in two-dimensional or three-dimensional space.

Well, that was helpful. The best way to understand transforms is to see them in action.

FIG 4.1: A grid of three hyperlinked photos.

So let's first walk through a simple example applying various 2D transforms on a small photo gallery. We'll then use those same techniques in practice on the moon example site later in the chapter.

THE SCALE TRANSFORM

Consider a horizontal list of three subtly framed photos from a recent trip to Martha's Vineyard, a small island off the coast of Massachusetts (FIG 4.1). This is a rather typical design pattern: a grid of linked images.

We're going to rely once again on our trusty unordered list to mark these up:

```
<ul class="gallery">
    <li><a href="#"><img src="photo-1.jpg" /></a></li>
    <li><a href="#"><img src="photo-2.jpg" /></a></li>
    <li><a href="#"><img src="photo-3.jpg" /></a></li>
</ul>
```

With no style yet applied, FIGURE 4.2 shows how this list would appear by default. Notice how the images are quite a bit larger than we'd like them to be in the final design. This is intentional, as we'll be using CSS to scale them down.

Adding style

Let's add some CSS to make this vertical list of photos a horizontal grid, with a one-pixel border around each image. (Also note the page background is a light gray #eee.)

FIG 4.2: The list of large photos, before CSS is applied.

```
ul.gallery li {
    float: left;
    margin: 0 10px;
    padding: 10px;
    border: 1px solid #ddd;
    list-style: none;
}

ul.gallery li a img {
    float: left;
    width: 200px;
}
```

Here we've floated the list items, turned `list-style` bullets off, and wrapped each `li` in a one-pixel gray border. We've also floated the images themselves and sized them down to 200 pixels wide. Those two compact declarations will get us where we want to go in terms of a default design (refer back to **FIG 4.1**).

Applying the scale transform on hover

Now it's time for transforms. Let's add a `scale` transform to make the photo larger when hovered. Remember that the original images in the markup are larger than the 200-pixel width we're specifying in the stylesheet. That means we can safely scale up the photo while maintaining its quality.

Scale transforms are supported in Safari, Chrome, Firefox, and Opera—each requiring a vendor prefix—as well as IE, which doesn't require a prefix. Let's add a stack that satisfies those browsers as well as any future ones.

```
ul.gallery li a:hover img {
  -webkit-transform: scale(1.5);
  -moz-transform: scale(1.5);
  -o-transform: scale(1.5);
  transform: scale(1.5);
}
```

When the hyperlinks are hovered, we're saying, "scale the images to 1.5 times their initial size" (which was 200px wide). Setting `scale(2)` would make the photo twice as large, `scale(0.5)` would make it half as large, etc.

FIGURE 4.3 shows the result, viewed here in Safari. Notice how the `transform` doesn't disturb the rest of the elements in the document, and zooms the photo out from the center, without affecting the layout around it.

You can also optionally set a `transform-origin` that will dictate where the scaling will expand from: top, bottom, center, or a percentage (see http://bkaprt.com/css3-2/11/).

For example, to have the photo scale out from the bottom left of its container instead of the center, you'd write this:

FIG 4.3: The middle photo being hovered and scaled with a CSS transform.

```
ul.gallery li a:hover img {
    -webkit-transform-origin: bottom left;
    -moz-transform-origin: bottom left;
    -o-transform-origin: bottom left;
    transform-origin: bottom left;
    -webkit-transform: scale(1.5);
    -moz-transform: scale(1.5);
    -o-transform: scale(1.5);
    transform: scale(1.5);
}
```

An appropriate drop shadow

We could go a step further with this example and add a drop shadow to the photo when hovered. This would be an appropriate use of the CSS3 box-shadow property, as we're making the enlarged photo appear as if it's pulling up off the page.

Now, the drop shadow is a delicate beast, an often-overused crutch by the trigger-happy designer. It's easy to get carried away and overdo it. But in this case, we're attempting to add *dimension* to the photo enlargement, so it should work out quite well.

The syntax for box-shadow is identical to the text-shadow property we used back in Chapter 3. However, unlike text-shadow, box-shadow requires vendor prefixes in order to work in older versions of Safari, Chrome, and Firefox. (Opera 10+ and IE9+ support the non-prefixed box-shadow.) Let's fold those rules in.

FIG 4.4: The hovered photo, now scaled with box-shadow applied.

```
ul.gallery li a:hover img {
  -webkit-transform: scale(1.5);
  -moz-transform: scale(1.5);
  -o-transform: scale(1.5);
  transform: scale(1.5);
  -webkit-box-shadow: 4px 4px 10px rgba(0, 0, 0, 0.5);
  -moz-box-shadow: 4px 4px 10px rgba(0, 0, 0, 0.5);
  box-shadow: 4px 4px 10px rgba(0, 0, 0, 0.5);
}
```

We've added a CSS3 stack for the box-shadow property for the older versions of WebKit and Mozilla browsers, ending with the non-prefixed version as we have with other examples.

In terms of the syntax, here we're applying a shadow on the hovered image that is 4px from the top, 4px from the left, has a 10px blur, and is black at 50% opacity (ensuring it'll blend in to whatever background or element sits behind it).

FIGURE 4.4 shows the shadow now appearing in conjunction with the scale transform when a photo is hovered over. This combination gives the effect of having the enlarged photo pop out from the page.

Smoothing out the zoom with a transition

Lastly, adding a transition to the linked photos will smooth out the scaling, giving the :hover treatment an animated zoom-in-and-out—an effect previously only possible with Flash or JavaScript, but now possible in many browsers with just the few lines of CSS3.

Here's the transition stack added to the complete CSS for our little photo gallery:

```
ul.gallery li {
    float: left;
    margin: 0 10px;
    padding: 10px;
    border: 1px solid #ddd;
    list-style: none;
}

ul.gallery li a img {
    float: left;
    width: 200px;
    -webkit-transition:
        -webkit-transform 0.2s ease-in-out;
    -moz-transition:
        -moz-transform 0.2s ease-in-out;
    transition: transform 0.2s ease-in-out;
}
ul.gallery li a:hover img {
    -webkit-transform: scale(1.5);
    -moz-transform: scale(1.5);
    -o-transform: scale(1.5);
    transform: scale(1.5);
    -webkit-box-shadow: 4px 4px 10px rgba(0, 0, 0, 0.5);
    -moz-box-shadow: 4px 4px 10px rgba(0, 0, 0, 0.5);
    box-shadow: 4px 4px 10px rgba(0, 0, 0, 0.5);
}
```

Notice this time, the property we're transitioning is the scale transform, hence the appropriate vendor prefixes are in place for both the transition and transform properties.

TRANSFORMING THE EXPERIENCE

With everything in place, the result is quite impressive for the minimal amount of CSS that's required to make it happen. We're putting most of the burden of the effect back on the browsers that support it, rather than injecting Flash or JavaScript to make it happen.

Again, the place where we chose to fully embrace CSS3 in this particular example is in the experience layer: when the photo is hovered, we're offering an enhanced view. It's not critical for browsers that don't support those properties.

Users of Internet Explorer, for example, will just see a gallery of clickable thumbnails, and that's perfectly OK. If the hover treatment were *critical,* then we'd need to rethink our use of CSS3 to achieve the visual experience.

ROTATE, SKEW, AND TRANSLATE

In addition to scale, there are three other transforms available for rotating, skewing, and translating elements. (Translate moves elements via x/y coordinates.) Let's add each to the photo gallery example to quickly see how they operate.

Adding rotation

If we wanted to rotate the photo when hovered, while still scaling it up, we can add the following rotate transform to the :hover rule:

```
ul.gallery li a:hover img {
    -webkit-transform: scale(1.5) rotate(-10deg);
    -moz-transform: scale(1.5) rotate(-10deg);
    -o-transform: scale(1.5) rotate(-10deg);
    transform: scale(1.5) rotate(-10deg);
    -webkit-box-shadow: 4px 4px 10px rgba(0, 0, 0, 0.5);
    -moz-box-shadow: 4px 4px 10px rgba(0, 0, 0, 0.5);
    box-shadow: 4px 4px 10px rgba(0, 0, 0, 0.5);
}
```

FIG 4.5: A hovered photo, now scaled and rotated to the left using the rotate transform.

FIG 4.6: Using rotate to make the photos appear scattered on the page.

We're still scaling up the photo on hover, but we're also tipping the photo 10 degrees to the left using rotate (**FIG 4.5**). A negative value from -1deg to -360deg rotates the element counter-clockwise, while a positive value from 1deg to 360deg rotates it clockwise.

Alternatively, we could add varying rotate transforms to the list items, so that the photo (and frame) appear to be tossed on

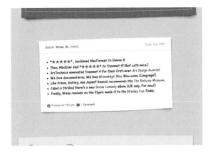

FIG 4.7: Panic Software's blog design uses subtle rotation via CSS3 to add realism.

FIG 4.8: Without rotation, the blog still looks great. Nothing appears missing or broken.

the table, randomly. Then we can rotate and scale on :hover as well (**FIG 4.6**).

I'm stressing in this little book that the most appropriate place to add CSS3 is on the experience layer—but that doesn't mean you can't use these techniques on the default view of a design, provided again that they're not critical and degrade well.

For example, should the browser not support rotate transforms, and the photos appear perfectly straight, that would be fine. Nothing would appear broken.

No rotate? Don't Panic

Panic Software's blog has a nice example of using rotate in the primary design of a page (http://www.panic.com/blog), where they use very subtle rotation via CSS3 to tip the entries to the left as if they're sheets of paper left on a desk (**FIG 4.7**). It's not crucial to the design, and if the entries are straight without rotation (**FIG 4.8**), it's perfectly OK.

FIG 4.9: The Outside iPhone app uses rotation on the sun graphic.

FIG 4.10: Outside app's sun graphic comes to life after positioning and rotating with CSS.

Rotating the sun

Another nice example of an appropriate use of CSS transforms is the site for Outside (http://outsideapp.com), a wonderful weather app for the iPhone (FIG 4.9).

At the top of the page is a sun graphic (FIG 4.10) that rotates 360° via the use of the rotate transform. (In this case, JavaScript

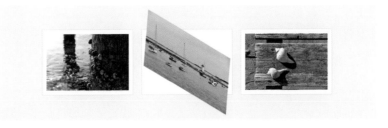

FIG 4.11: Using the skew transform to distort the photo.

is used to animate the rotation in non-WebKit browsers, but we'll be discussing pure CSS-based animations later in Chapter 6). This subtle experience enhancement is simple and appropriate, as it mimics the same animated sunshine that appears in the iPhone app itself. The sun doesn't rotate in browsers that don't support CSS transforms, and that's perfectly fine. Nothing appears broken or missing in a non-animated version of the site.

Transforms coupled with transitions in CSS can help support the overall message in the designs we create for the web, and that's a wonderfully enabling tool for us web designers.

The skew transform

The skew transform takes x and y coordinates and skews an element. If we were to skew the photos in our gallery on hover, for example, we'd use the following CSS (skewing negative five degrees on the x coordinate, and 30 degrees on the y coordinate) (**FIG 4.11**):

```
ul.gallery li a:hover img {
    -webkit-transform: scale(1.5) skew(-5deg, 30deg);
    -moz-transform: scale(1.5) skew(-5deg, 30deg);
    -o-transform: scale(1.5) skew(-5deg, 30deg);
    transform: scale(1.5) skew(-5deg, 30deg);
}
```

FIG 4.12: Skewing the photo 30 degrees on both the x and y axis.

Like rotate, skew accepts positive and negative degree values. You can also use just one value for both x and y like so (FIG 4.12):

```
ul.gallery li a:hover img {
    -webkit-transform: scale(1.5) skew(30deg);
    -moz-transform: scale(1.5) skew(30deg);
    -o-transform: scale(1.5) skew(30deg);
    transform: scale(1.5) skew(30deg);
}
```

Now I realize that what we just did to the photo is far from visually compelling, and admittedly, I don't use skew all that often; however, I'm convinced there are interesting uses for it.

For example, skew could be used on blocks of text to create three-dimensional visuals—all with semantic markup and CSS3 (FIGS 4.13 and 4.14).

The translate transform

Lastly, the translate transform allows you to *move* an element from its normal position on screen, using x and y coordinates.

For example, if we wanted to move an image in the photo gallery from its initial position upon hover, we could do that with translate. And with our transition in place, that movement will be smoothly animated.

Here's the syntax for moving the image 20 pixels to the right and 40 pixels from the top of its original location (FIG 4.15):

FIG 4.13: A demo by Paul Hayes using skew and transitions to create multiple 3D cubes from simple chunks of hypertext (http://www.paulrhayes .com/experiments/cube/multiCubes .html).

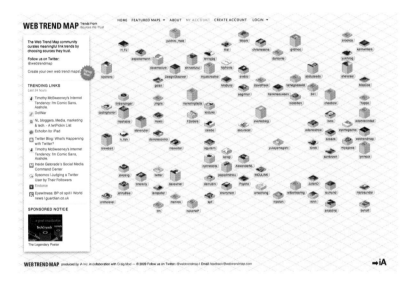

FIG 4.14: The Web Trend Map uses skew to place avatars on an isometric grid, creating unique data visualizations from otherwise flat elements (http://webtrendmap.com).

FIG 4.15: Using the translate transform to move the photo on :hover.

```
ul.gallery li a:hover img {
    -webkit-transform: scale(1.5) translate(20px, 40px);
    -moz-transform: scale(1.5) translate(20px, 40px);
    -o-transform: scale(1.5) translate(20px, 40px);
    transform: scale(1.5) translate(20px, 40px);
}
```

If we wanted to move the image to the left and/or top, we'd use negative values, e.g., translate(-20px, -40px).

Like the aforementioned transforms, translate doesn't disturb the other elements in the document, moving it explicitly to wherever you tell it to go. That means you don't have to be concerned with margins, padding, clearing floats, or absolute positioning. Give an element translate coordinates and it'll move it there.

DIFFERENT TRANSFORMS TO HELP SUPPORT THE STORY

The photo gallery example demonstrated how scale, rotate, skew, and translate can work together with transitions to create richer experiences. The key to using these transforms well is to find appropriate situations in which they'll assist in telling the story of what's on screen.

Again, it's easy to get carried away with transforms, because, well, they're fun and simple to implement. But searching for the

FIG 4.16: The slideshow carousel area of *Things We Left on the Moon.*

appropriate places in the experience layer to enable them will make for a better end product.

TRANSFORMING THE MOON

Let's return to the moon example site, where I've used various transforms and transitions to help liven up the experience on the slideshow gallery (**FIG 4.16**).

When hovering each of the items left on the moon, the image reacts in a different way, depending on the nature of the item being featured, be it a doughnut, a lawnmower, a cat, etc.

Adding an appropriate transform/transition to each of the items is not only fun and easy to implement, it's also harmless for browsers that don't yet support the bits of CSS3 that make the interaction possible.

Let's go through each item one by one to see how scale, rotate, positioning, and opacity can be combined with transitions to complete the experience.

Supporting the message

If we think about each of the linked items, and specifically about their *meaning,* we can then apply a transform and/or transition that supports the story of the object at hand.

How would a big doughnut or reclining chair react to interaction? We can choose to apply the appropriate CSS3 here to help enrich the experience (**FIG 4.17**).

The markup

To mark up this faux carousel of wacky things, the semantics are quite simple: just an ordered list of linked images, with a heading underneath to describe what each item is.

```
<ol id="things">
  <li id="things-1">
    <a href="#"><img src="img/doughnut.png" /></a>
    <h2>1 big doughnut</h2>
  </li>
  <li id="things-2">
    <a href="#"><img src="img/mower.png" /></a>
    <h2>1 lawnmower</h2>
  </li>
  <li id="things-3">
    <a href="#"><img src="img/cat.png" /></a>
    <h2>1 astro cat</h2>
  </li>
  <li id="things-4">
    <a href="#"><img src="img/recliner.png" /></a>
    <h2>1 recliner</h2>
  </li>
  <li id="things-5">
    <a href="#"><img src="img/gnome.png" /></a>
    <h2>1 magic gnome</h2>
  </li>
</ol>
```

Notice we've added an id of #things to the list itself, and then an id for each list item as well, so that we can add unique interactions to the :hover state of each item.

Base styles for each item

Next we'll add the base CSS for each list item that contains the linked images. The following styles float the items to make them horizontal, set relative positioning for the context in which

FIG 4.17: The things we'll be transforming.

we will later absolutely position each image, and finally, add a rounded, semi-transparent background frame.

```
ol#things li {
    position: relative;
    float: left;
    margin: 0 15px 0 0;
    padding: 10px;
    background: #444; /* backup for non-RGBA */
    background: rgba(255, 255, 255, 0.1);
    list-style: none;
    -webkit-border-radius: 4px;
    -moz-border-radius: 4px;
    -o-border-radius: 4px;
    border-radius: 4px;
}
```

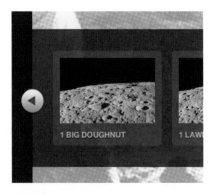

FIG 4.18: The list items, now with the moon background image.

We'll now set the moon background image that appears behind each item, as well as giving each link a specific width and height (**FIG 4.18**).

```
ol#things li a {
    float: left;
    width: 137px;
    height: 91px;
    background: url(../img/moon-137.jpg) »
      no-repeat top left;
}
```

Catch-all declaration

Our next step is to create a catch-all declaration that will absolutely position each image within the list item's frame and therefore on top of the moon background image.

We'll be positioning each item slightly differently depending on the object, as well as using varying transforms, but we can declare position: absolute; here for *all* images so we don't have to duplicate that rule for each item. We'll also add a transition stack using the all value. That way, any transform or change we wish to make on each thing will be transitioned and smoothed out, regardless of which CSS properties we decide to change.

```
ol#things li a img {
  position: absolute;
  -webkit-transition: all 0.2s ease-in;
  -moz-transition: all 0.2s ease-in;
  -o-transition: all 0.2s ease-in;
  transition: all 0.2s ease-in;
}
```

Now we're ready to add exact positioning and width for each image, taking advantage of those ids we added to each list item.

```
ol#things li#things-1 a img {
  width: 60px;
  top: 23px;
  left: 26px;
}

ol#things li#things-2 a img {
  width: 50px;
  top: 20px;
  left: 50px;
}

ol#things li#things-3 a img {
  width: 80px;
  top: 19px;
  left: 30px;
}

ol#things li#things-4 a img {
  width: 70px;
  top: 25px;
  left: 45px;
}
```

```
ol#things li#things-5 a img {
  width: 80px;
  top: 20px;
  left: 34px;
  }
```

I've created these images on the large side, so that if we wish to scale them up, we can do so without stretching the image beyond its native dimensions.

Now we'll add a unique :hover treatment to each item, knowing that the catch-all transition will smooth out and animate whatever we fold in.

Scaling the big doughnut

The big doughnut gets bigger on hover, so we'll use the scale transform here to scale up the image. Remember that the original image in the markup is quite a bit bigger than what we sized down to in the stylesheet. This was intentional, so we could scale it up like this.

```
ol#things li#things-1 a:hover img {
  -webkit-transform: scale(1.25);
  -moz-transform: scale(1.25);
  -o-transform: scale(1.25);
  transform: scale(1.25);
  }
```

These rules will scale the doughnut up by 25% on hover. **FIGURE 4.19** shows the normal and hover states, with the doughnut getting a little bigger when moused over.

Perspective with scale and position

For the lawnmower left on the moon, we'll do two things:

FIG 4.19: The big doughnut gets bigger on :hover using scale.

1. Scale it larger with a transform.
2. Move it down and to the right.

These two changes plus the transition make the mower appear like it's coming at you. (Look out!) It's very subtle, but simple and effective.

We'll adjust the default position five pixels lower and 10 pixels to the right. And we'll also add a transform stack to scale the mower 20% larger than the default.

```
ol#things li#things-2 a:hover img {
    top: 25px;
    left: 60px;
    -webkit-transform: scale(1.2);
    -moz-transform: scale(1.2);
    -o-transform: scale(1.2);
    transform: scale(1.2);
}
```

FIGURE 4.20 shows the default and hovered state, and the illusion of a mower coming at you is complete.

FIG 4.20: The lawnmower uses position and scale to create a pseudo three-dimensional effect.

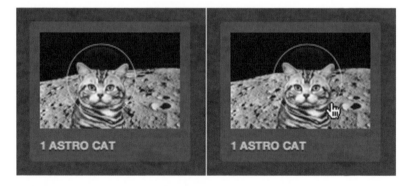

FIG 4.21: The cat slides back and forth, as cats often do.

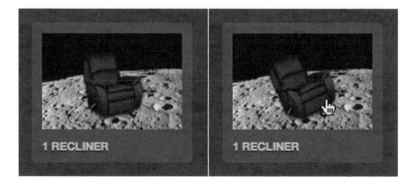

FIG 4.22: The recliner tips back to the left using a negative value on the rotate transform.

The elusive astro cat

We can add CSS transitions on a whole host of properties (not just CSS3 ones); simply smoothing out a *position* change can make the astro cat appear as though it's avoiding the mouse. By adjusting the `left` position of the image on hover, the catch-all transition will smooth that movement out, making the astro cat appear like it's sliding back and forth.

Here we'll move the cat 15 pixels to the right by upping the `left` value from `30px` to `45px` (**FIG 4.21**):

```
ol#things li#things-3 a:hover img {
  left: 45px;
}
```

Pretty simple. And it's really the CSS transition that's doing the magic here (which is difficult to illustrate on a sheet of pressed wood pulp).

Tipping back the recliner

A good recliner tips back, and we can mimic that real-world reaction with the aforementioned `rotate` transform.

Let's add the transform stack to rotate the recliner slightly, to the left. We'll use the vendor-prefixed rules for WebKit, Mozilla, and Opera-based browsers, as well as ending with the actual `transform` property for future implementations.

```
ol#things li#things-4 a:hover img {
  -webkit-transform: rotate(-15deg);
  -moz-transform: rotate(-15deg);
  -o-transform: rotate(-15deg);
  transform: rotate(-15deg);
}
```

We used a *negative* value to tip the image to the left (counterclockwise), and once again the transition will smooth out that subtle rotation, completing the illusion of our comfy, plushy chair on the moon (**FIG 4.22**).

FIG 4.23: The gnome *almost* disappears by reducing opacity on :hover.

The disappearing gnome

For the final item, we'll take a lounging gnome and make him partially disappear. Somehow, that seems like a perfectly natural thing for a gnome to do.

We'll use the opacity property to simply and quickly create a hover style for the image, dimming it down considerably. Because of the transition already in place for all property changes on the image, the opacity swap will animate in browsers that support transitions, creating a smooth disappearance for our little friend.

The declaration is simply:

```
ol#things li#things-5 a:hover img {
    opacity: 0.4;
}
```

FIGURE 4.23 shows how the gnome fades out to 40% opacity on :hover.

Harmless degradation

Like the photo gallery example we discussed earlier in the chapter, the sprinkling of CSS3 we're adding here is harmless for browsers that don't yet support it.

FIG 4.24: An attempt to convey on paper the chaos that results from the "rotate everything on hover" trick.

In the end, the important thing here is that each of these items is a clickable link. What happens beyond that is an enriched experience for those that are capable of receiving it.

ONE MORE TIME NOW: BE SMART, BE SUBTLE

By taking a little time to think about the *meaning* behind the content we're dealing with, we can choose to apply some of the CSS3 properties that work today along with transitions and transforms.

These experience enhancements can be the mark of a true web craftsperson: attention to details that not everyone will notice, care and feeding for non-critical visual events, and elevating the message a step beyond the norm. For browsers that support this stuff now, and those that will in the future, the small amount of code and thought is well worth it.

Try and be subtle when it comes to CSS transforms. It's easy to get carried away, but when used appropriately, they can make all the difference in the way the reader experiences the message you're delivering.

More "wow," please

Speaking of getting carried away, the next time your client or boss says, "this design needs more 'wow'" or "it's missing some pizzazz!" just add the following declaration to your stylesheet (and make sure they're using Safari, Chrome, Firefox, or Opera, of course):

```
*:hover {
    -webkit-transform: rotate(180deg);
    -moz-transform: rotate(180deg);
    -o-transform: rotate(180deg);
    transform: rotate(180deg);
}
```

This little bit of CSS3 says, "hover over *anything* on the page, and rotate it 180 degrees." Try it. It's a sure-fire way to make a big impression (**FIG 4.24**).

Actually, the sad thing is that there are some clients and bosses that might *love* this.

"This is great! Ship it!"

Sigh.

5 MULTIPLE BACKGROUNDS

IF YOU ASKED ME two years ago, "What's the one thing you're looking most forward to in CSS3?" I might've enthusiastically replied, "Multiple background images!" At the time, the ability to layer more than one background image on a single element seemed as though it would cure a lot of the headaches we'd been suffering as web designers.

To create flexible, bulletproof solutions to design problems, we must figure out how we can get by using fewer graphics or without adding extraneous markup as hooks for extra background images. We've done the best with what we've had, but the promise of being able to assign multiple background images to an element had always seemed, to me, to be this wonderful promise of easier times with less code.

The reality, though, is that along the way, browsers have added support for much of the Backgrounds and Borders Module in CSS3 (http://bkaprt.com/css3-2/12/). Many of the properties we've discussed previously in the book have decent browser support today in Safari, Chrome, Firefox, Opera, and

FIG 5.1: The background of the moon example site, where four PNGs are stacked to create a sense of deep space.

IE. And properties like border-radius, box-shadow, gradients, RGBA, and opacity make it possible to solve common problems without images at all. Many of the techniques that previously required images are possible entirely within the stylesheets themselves. All of that has obvious benefits.

So while a few years ago I was salivating over the prospect of multiple background support, today I'm less excited because of all the other tools we have at our disposal. That said, there are *wonderful* use cases for assigning multiple background images on a single element, and we're going to talk about one particular technique in this brief chapter.

PARALLAX SCROLLING

If we take a look back at the moon example site, I've used multiple background images on the body element to create a layered space environment. Instead of one flat image, there are four semi-transparent PNGs stacked on top of each other. Each has its own horizontal positioning to create an animated effect when the browser window is resized (**FIG 5.1**).

This technique of speed-shifting layers has been dubbed "parallax scrolling," which our friends at Wikipedia (http://bkaprt.com/css3-2/13/) define as:

> *A special scrolling technique in computer graphics, seen first in the 1982 arcade game Moon Patrol. In this pseudo-3D technique, background images move by the "camera" slower than*

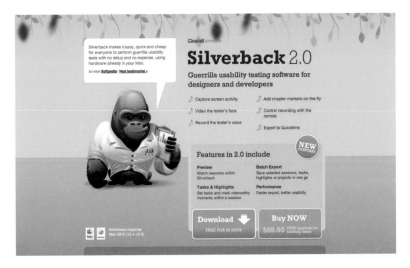

FIG 5.2: Resize the browser window while visiting Silverback and enjoy the three-dimensional jungle experience.

foreground images, creating an illusion of depth in a 2D video game and adding to the immersion. The technique grew out of the multiplane camera technique used in traditional animation since the 1940s.

Many great examples of applying the parallax effect on the web have been popping up over the last few years, and a long-time favorite of mine is the site for Silverback (http://silverback-app.com), a handy piece of usability testing software from the folks at Clearleft (**FIG 5.2**).

Resize the browser window back and forth and notice how the layers of vines hanging down from the top shift back and forth at slightly different speeds, creating a sense of dimension. (I did that for probably an hour straight when I first encountered the site.).

Sure, not everyone is going to see it—but for those that *do* experience it, it's a wonderful detail and enhanced user experience that can't help but make you just a tiny bit happier.

THE OLD WAY: EXTRA MARKUP

So how is it done? Paul Annett wrote up the techniques he used to create the parallax effect specifically for the Silverback site in an article for *Think Vitamin* back in early 2008 (http://bkaprt.com/css3-2/14/).

To layer the three layers of vines, each a separate PNG, you must have at least three available block-level elements. Two extra wrapper divs are necessary to place a background image on the body, #midground, and #foreground elements.

I'm loosely translating here, for simplicity, but the markup would be something like:

```
<body>
  <div id="midground">
    <div id="foreground">
      <!-- page content here -->
    </div>
  </div>
</body>
```

The CSS to place the three images, each with varying horizontal positions, would be something like:

```
body {
  background: url(vines-back.png) repeat-x 20% 0;
}

#midground {
  background: url(vines-mid.png) repeat-x 40% 0;
}

#foreground {
  background: url(vines-front.png) repeat-x 150% 0;
}
```

Now this works perfectly well. But it's made far simpler when using the multiple backgrounds syntax introduced in CSS3.

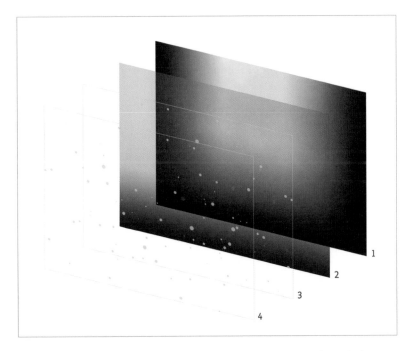

FIG 5.3: The four semi-transparent background PNGs that are layered underneath the moon example site.

Let's take a look at how multiple backgrounds are applied to the body of the moon example site, and how that creates a simpler parallax effect for those that might experience it.

THE NEW WAY: MULTIPLE BACKGROUNDS VIA CSS3

I'm using four semi-transparent PNGs to create the deep space background used on the moon example site. They're all layered on the body element, stacked one on top of each other to create that sense of dimension when the user resizes the browser window.

FIGURE 5.3 shows each of the four PNG images used:

1. Dust clouds (clouds.png)
2. Blue to purple gradient (space-bg.png)
3. Layer of stars (stars-1.png)
4. Another layer of randomly-placed stars (stars-2.png)

Multiple backgrounds syntax

And here's how simple it is to assign these four images as backgrounds of the body element, using the updated CSS3 syntax:

```
body {
  background:
    url(../img/stars-1.png) repeat-x fixed -130% 0,
    url(../img/stars-2.png) repeat-x fixed 40% 0,
    url(../img/space-bg.png) repeat-x fixed -80% 0,
    url(../img/clouds.png) repeat-x fixed 100% 0;
  background-color: #1a1a1a;
}
```

Here I'm layering the four images, with the clouds at the bottom and stars on top in a comma-delimited list. (Notice the stacking order starts with the image "closest" to the user.) I'm also repeating each of these horizontally, and setting them at differing horizontal positions (using positive and negative values) to make each layer "shift" at different speeds as the window is resized. And finally, I've fixed them in a locked position on the page with the fixed value.

The almost-black background color of #1a1a1a is added in last as a separate background-color rule.

And that's it (**FIG 5.4**). What's wonderful about this is that there is no extraneous markup necessary. We're putting all of these images on the body element so that they'll sit behind the page's content, but we didn't need to add dummy wrapper divs to layer them.

What about browser support?

As mentioned back in Chapter 1, multiple backgrounds are supported in Safari 1.3+, Chrome 2+, Firefox 3.6+, Opera 10.5+,

FIG 5.4: The four PNGs layered on top of each other as well as a dark charcoal background color.

and IE9+. So, really, they're on par with many of the other CSS properties we've been using throughout the book.

Once again, we've chosen to utilize this wonderful CSS3 gem in a non-critical part of the design because of that imperfect support: enriching the *background* of the page, heightening the experience of resizing the window by creating a parallax effect for those that are able to experience it.

Providing a fallback for all browsers

Older browsers that don't support multiple backgrounds will ignore the entire `background` rule. And that's precisely why we've defined the `background-color` in a separate rule.

FIGURE 5.5 shows the moon example site as viewed in IE7, where the multiple background images we've declared are ignored, showing only the charcoal `background-color`.

Now, nothing is *broken* here—but losing all the space-y-ness in the background is a shame. The solution is to specify a single fallback background image *first* in the declaration, for browsers

FIG 5.5: IE7 ignores the rule where multiple background images are declared, showing only the dark charcoal background color.

(like IE7 and 8) that don't support multiple images. Then we can override that rule with the multiple one (which will be ignored by IE).

```
body {
  background: url(../img/space-bg.png) »
    repeat-x fixed -80% 0;
  background:
    url(../img/stars-1.png) repeat-x fixed -130% 0,
    url(../img/stars-2.png) repeat-x fixed 40% 0,
    url(../img/space-bg.png) repeat-x fixed -80% 0,
    url(../img/clouds.png) repeat-x fixed 100% 0;
  background-color: #1a1a1a;
}
```

For the single image fallback, you could choose one of the images used in the multiple declaration, or even go so far as to create a flattened version of the multiple layers.

For the moon site, I've chosen to simply use `space-bg.png`, which is the color gradient image (FIG 5.6), therefore serving a starless, cloudless version of the background to browsers that don't yet support multiple background images. How appropriate.

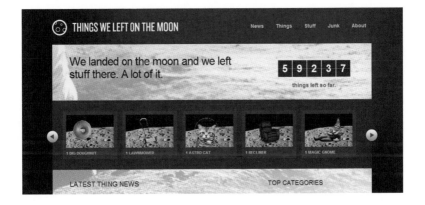

FIG 5.6: With the single fallback image in place, IE7 now has a bit more space-y-ness restored.

USING MULTIPLE BACKGROUNDS TODAY

In keeping with the theme of the other examples in the book, here we're using multiple background images today. We're forging ahead with a CSS3 property that has healthy support in Safari, Chrome, Firefox, Opera, and IE. Instead of fearing the non-support in older browser versions, we're choosing to apply the property on a non-critical visual event (a parallax-shifting background).

We also know that if the browser doesn't support multiple backgrounds, it will ignore the entire background rule. To compensate, we'll define a flat or alternate single graphic in a background rule that comes before the multiple one.

And with all of that in mind, we can now more flexibly experiment with layering, shifting, and positioning background images on top of each other, without the need for extra markup. It'll be exciting to see how this technique is used in creative new ways.

6 ENRICHING FORMS

FORMS ARE ANOTHER ASPECT of a website that can involve interaction, and therefore they offer additional visual events that are ripe for enriching with CSS3.

By default, form elements themselves can differ drastically in appearance depending on the browser or operating system in which they're viewed. Why not embrace that variation by choosing to apply the portions of CSS3 that work today to heighten the experience?

It's important to strike a balance between subtle modification of form elements and maintaining the familiar to ensure usability for your forms. In other words, an input should still obviously appear as an input. Now that CSS is capable of deep styling of form elements (in most browsers), we have to be careful not to tamper with the most important part: the functionality.

That said, there's a lot we *can* do with forms in regards to CSS3 to enrich the experience for browsers that support it now, while degrading that experience gracefully for browsers that don't.

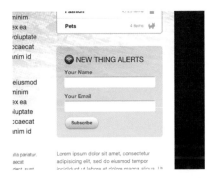

This chapter also gives us an excuse to talk about three portions of CSS3 that we haven't yet touched on:

1. Powerful new selectors
2. CSS Gradients
3. CSS Animations

Again, we'll use the moon example site as a launching pad to talk about how forms and CSS3 can work together in new and creative ways; specifically, the "New Thing Alerts" sign-up form that sits in the right sidebar (FIG 6.1).

MARKING UP THE SIMPLE SIGN-UP FORM

In terms of HTML, this little form is about as simple as it gets. Just a few inputs with labels and a submit button.

```
<form action="/" id="thing-alerts">
  <fieldset>
    <label for="alerts-name">Your Name</label>
    <input type="text" id="alerts-name"  />
  </fieldset>

  <fieldset>
    <label for="alerts-email">Your Email</label>
    <input type="email" id="alerts-email" />
  </fieldset>
```

FIG 6.2: The form viewed in Safari, sans styles.

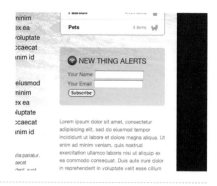

```
    <fieldset>
      <input type="submit" value="Subscribe" />
    </fieldset>
  </form>
```

FIGURE 6.2 shows the form with the default browser styles (as viewed in Safari).

ADDING STYLES FOR FIELDSET AND LABEL

The first bits of CSS we'll add to start sculpting this form are for the fieldset and label elements—just a bit of spacing between each row.

```
#thing-alerts fieldset {
  margin: 0 0 10px 0;
}

#thing-alerts label {
  display: block;
  font-weight: bold;
  line-height: 1.4;
  color: #666;
  color: rgba(0, 0, 0, 0.6);
  text-shadow: 0 1px 1px #fff;
}
```

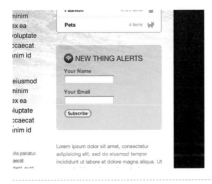

FIG 6.3: The fieldset and label elements are now styled.

Looking at **FIGURE 6.3** you'll notice we've added a 10px margin below each fieldset row, and we've set labels to display: block to put them on their own line. We've also assigned black at 60% transparency for the text, as well as a backup color of solid gray for browsers that don't yet support RGBA. And we've applied a subtle white highlight with text-shadow, to make the text appear as though it's inset on the background.

Now while we have nice 10-pixel spacing between fieldset rows, because of the padding inside the gray box, we *don't* need the 10-pixel margin under the last row (containing the submit button).

This is a common pattern: you have a list or succession of elements, each with the same styles applied, but you'd like to style the last element in that succession a little differently.

Instead of adding class="last" to the final element, why not take advantage of the :last-child pseudo-class in CSS3 to remove the bottom margin without having to touch the markup:

```
#thing-alerts fieldset {
  margin: 0 0 10px 0;
}

#thing-alerts fieldset label {
  display: block;
  font-weight: bold;
  line-height: 1.4;
```

FIG 6.4: With the bottom margin removed from the final `fieldset`, our form spacing is looking good.

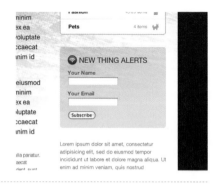

```
    color: #666;
    color: rgba(0, 0, 0, 0.6);
    text-shadow: 0 1px 1px #fff;
}

#thing-alerts fieldset:last-child {
    margin: 0;
}
```

Keep in mind that `:last-child` isn't supported in IE8 and below, but for minor presentational adjustments like this one, it's a great alternative to adding a class in the markup.

FIGURE 6.4 shows where we're at currently, now with bottom margin on the last `fieldset` element removed by way of the `:last-child` pseudo-class.

More CSS3 selectors

While we're making good use of `:last-child`, it's a good time to point out that there are many more wonderfully convenient new selectors in CSS3.

I highly recommend Roger Johansson's article on the subject, "CSS3 selectors explained" (http://bkaprt.com/css3-2/15/) where he demonstrates what they are and how they work. Support for CSS3 selectors varies across browsers, so be sure to reference Peter-Paul Koch's thorough "CSS contents and browser compatibility" tables (http://bkaprt.com/css3-2/16/) and "CSS

Compatibility and Internet Explorer" from Microsoft (http://bkaprt.com/css3-2/17/) to see who supports what.

STYLING THE TEXT INPUTS

Next, let's start adding the styles that turn default text inputs into something a bit more customized. This time we'll use a CSS2.1 attribute selector to target the input type="text" elements only (and not the input type="submit" button).

If we simply declared:

```
#thing-alerts input
```

we'd be styling all inputs in the form (text *and* buttons), but if we modify that to:

```
#thing-alerts input[type="text"]
```

we'll target the text inputs only.

Again, using a powerful selector in the stylesheet avoids having to add extra classes in the markup to style the various form elements separately. This is beautiful.

Keep in mind that while attribute selectors are supported in IE7 and above, they *aren't* supported in IE6, but that's OK since we're just modifying the non-critical appearance of these form elements. IE6 will ignore these rules, and that's perfectly acceptable in this case.

The following declaration applies a specific width, padding, and font-size, turns off default borders, adds a background-color, and rounds the corners of the inputs using our trusty border-radius stack.

```
#thing-alerts fieldset input[type="text"] {
    width: 215px;
    padding: 5px 8px;
    font-size: 1.2em;
    color: #666;
    border: none;
    background-color: #fff;
```

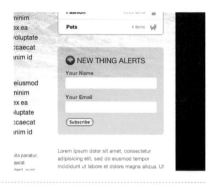

```
-webkit-border-radius: 4px;
-moz-border-radius: 4px;
-o-border-radius: 4px;
border-radius: 4px;
}
```

FIGURE 6.5 shows our progress viewed in Safari (with similar results in other recent browsers). We now have flat, rounded text inputs, which look quite nice, but let's add some depth to make them look more like a typical, editable input.

USING CSS3 GRADIENTS

One crafty way we can add some of that depth is by way of CSS gradients, which are new in CSS3. That is, create a gradient from one color to another without the use of any images. That sounds pretty enticing, doesn't it?

CSS gradients are supported in Safari 4+, Chrome 2+, Firefox 3.6+, Opera 20+, and IE 10+, but again, for non-critical uses, it can be a flexible solution that degrades well.

CSS gradients can be assigned anywhere that an image can be declared in the stylesheet; in other words, background-image, list-style-image, border-image, and generated content.

The syntax for declaring CSS gradients differs slightly between Safari's implementation and Firefox. The (very preliminary) spec, however, leans more toward the way Firefox handles things. Here's a prime example of why vendor prefixing is an important part of the process: these two varying syntaxes can be correctly declared for each browser, while the official spec is still being hashed out.

I'll be honest in saying that the syntax for either can be a tad bit confusing. There's an immense amount of control possible in creating gradients, including the colors involved, color stops, direction of the gradient, etc.

For example, here is the syntax for creating a simple linear gradient for both WebKit and Mozilla-based browsers on the background of an element:

```
#foo {
  background-image: -webkit-gradient(linear,»
    0% 0%, 0% 100%, from(#fff), to(#999));
  background-image: -moz-linear-gradient(0% 100%»
    90deg, #fff, #999);
}
```

It's not entirely intuitive, and it's also difficult to remember the differences for each vendor.

The best way I've found to come up with the right code is to use John Allsopp's wonderful WYSIWYG editor (**FIG 6.6**, http://bkaprt.com/css3-2/18/).

Use this tool to visually create the gradients you want, then grab the appropriate syntax for both Safari and Firefox. John's tool does all the heavy lifting for you. And this is extremely helpful as I haven't been able to memorize the code (and the differences between browsers) yet.

Jonathan Snook has a helpful post on working your way through gradient syntax that might prove helpful as well: http://bkaprt.com/css3-2/19/.

The gradient we want to add to our text inputs is very subtle—just a little lip to make it look inset (**FIG 6.7**). After fiddling and entering some values into John Allsopp's tool, we come up with two short lines of CSS:

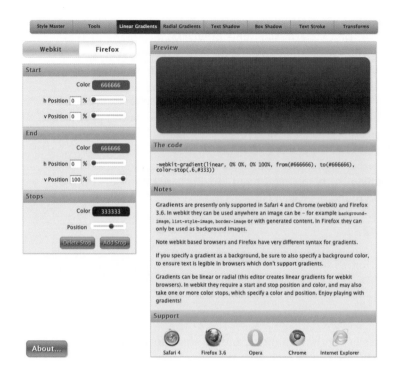

FIG 6.6: The wonderful CSS gradients tool by John Allsopp.

```
#thing-alerts fieldset input[type="text"] {
  width: 215px;
  padding: 5px 8px;
  font-size: 1.2em;
  color: #666;
  border: none;
  background-image: -webkit-gradient(linear, »
    0% 0%, 0% 12%, from(#999), to(#fff));
  background-image: -moz-linear-gradient(0% 12% »
    90deg, #fff, #999);
  background-color: #fff;
```

FIG 6.7: A zoomed view of the tiny gradient at the top of each text input that makes it look recessed.

```
    -webkit-border-radius: 4px;
    -moz-border-radius: 4px;
    -o-border-radius: 4px;
    border-radius: 4px;
}
```

We're applying a *linear* gradient here, but *radial* gradients are also possible with CSS.

And here you can see how the syntax differs between -webkit and -moz implementations. We're essentially adding a small linear gradient that goes from light gray (#999) to white (#fff) for just 12% of the vertical height of the input. We're applying the vendor-prefixed background-image rules to make that happen in Safari and Firefox.

FIGURE 6.8 shows the results, where you can see our rounded inputs now sporting a little inner shadow using no images.

Browsers that don't yet support CSS gradients will ignore those background-image rules and just be flat white. And that's perfectly fine. But the adjustment, flexibility, and control that come along with CSS gradients is rather compelling. We'll be using them a bit more in the next section regarding the submit button.

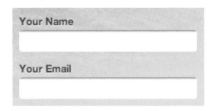

FIG 6.8: Text inputs with the CSS gradient in place.

A PURE CSS3 BUTTON

If there's one UI element that can demonstrate how transformative CSS3 can be, it just may be the button. Combining many of the techniques we've already discussed throughout the book, we'll turn an ordinary form submit button into something far more interesting—entirely with CSS (**FIG 6.9**).

The beauty of applying CSS3 to style the button is that by not using images, we're left with something far more flexible. If the browser doesn't support the properties we'll use to elevate this button visually, that's OK. It'll degrade nicely to a default form button in whatever browser the user happens to be using.

So let's walk through the steps needed to take a default form button to the wonderfully shiny one on the right in **FIGURE 6.9**.

Base button styles

First, we'll add some padding, change the font to Helvetica to match the rest of the design, turn off borders, and set the background color to white.

```
#thing-alerts input[type="submit"] {
    padding: 8px 15px;
    font-family: Helvetica, Arial, sans-serif;
    font-weight: bold;
    line-height: 1;
    color: #444;
    border: none;
    background-color: #fff;
}
```

FIGURE 6.10 shows how things are looking in Safari with those simple base styles applied. And we already have something that looks nothing like a default input button.

Rounding to a pill shape

Next, let's add a `border-radius` stack to get the button rounded down to a pill shape (**FIG 6.11**).

```
#thing-alerts fieldset input[type="submit"] {
    padding: 8px 15px;
    font-family: Helvetica, Arial, sans-serif;
    font-weight: bold;
    line-height: 1;
    color: #444;
    border: none;
    background-color: #fff;
    -webkit-border-radius: 50%;
    -moz-border-radius: 50%;
    border-radius: 50%;
}
```

FIG 6.11: Rounding the submit button using border-radius.

Assigning 50% radius will ensure those perfectly round corners, regardless of the font size.

Applying a linear gradient

Now let's apply a gradient of light gray (#bbb) from bottom up to white (#fff) at the top of the button. We'll again rely on Mr. Allsopp's gradient tool to spit out the correct rules for all browsers that support it.

```
#thing-alerts input[type="submit"] {
  padding: 8px 15px;
  font-family: Helvetica, Arial, sans-serif;
  font-weight: bold;
  line-height: 1;
  color: #444;
  border: none;
  background-image: -webkit-gradient(linear,»
    0% 0%, 0% 100%, from(#fff), to(#bbb));
  background-image: -moz-linear-gradient(0 100%»
    90deg, #bbb, #fff);
  background-color: #fff;
  -webkit-border-radius: 50%;
  -moz-border-radius: 50%;
  border-radius: 50%;
}
```

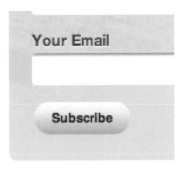

FIG 6.12: The CSS gradient added to the submit button.

FIGURE 6.12 shows the progress as viewed in Safari. Now we have a rounded button with a CSS gradient applied. So far, no images have been used and we've only added a few lines in our stylesheet.

Adding text-shadow to let the type sink in

Let's now add an almost-white `text-shadow` below the text that will make it look as if the text is stamped into the button.

```
#thing-alerts input[type="submit"] {
    padding: 8px 15px;
    font-family: Helvetica, Arial, sans-serif;
    font-weight: bold;
    line-height: 1;
    color: #444;
    border: none;
    text-shadow: 0 1px 1px rgba(255, 255, 255, 0.85);
    background-image: -webkit-gradient(linear, »
        0% 0%, 0% 100%, from(#fff), to(#bbb));
    background-image: -moz-linear-gradient(0 100% »
        90deg, #fff, #bbb);
    background-color: #fff;
    -webkit-border-radius: 50%;
    -moz-border-radius: 50%;
    border-radius: 50%;
}
```

FIG 6.13: A zoomed-in view of the
subtle text-shadow we added to create
an embossed look.

We'll use RGBA to tone down pure white to 85%, letting the gray gradient show through just a tiny bit. We're also specifying that the shadow sits directly under the text by one pixel, and blurring the shadow one pixel as well.

FIGURE 6.13 shows a close-up of the subtle shadow in place, as well as how the button is coming along so far.

Adding a box-shadow to the button

Our last piece of CSS3 to add to this stylish little button is a very slight `box-shadow` to add just another hint of dimension. It'll help it sit better on the gray background behind it.

Here's a stack that adds the box-shadow to the browsers that currently support it, as well as future ones.

```
#thing-alerts input[type="submit"] {
    padding: 8px 15px;
    font-family: Helvetica, Arial, sans-serif;
    font-weight: bold;
    line-height: 1;
    color: #444;
    border: none;
    text-shadow: 0 1px 1px rgba(255, 255, 255, 0.85);
    background-image: -webkit-gradient(linear, »
        0% 0%, 0% 100%, from(#fff), to(#bbb));
    background-image: -moz-linear-gradient(0% 100% »
        90deg, #bbb, #fff);
    background-color: #fff;
```

FIG 6.14: A zoomed-in view of the small box-shadow added to the bottom of the button, lifting it off the background just a bit.

```
-webkit-border-radius: 50%;
-moz-border-radius: 50%;
border-radius: 50%;
-webkit-box-shadow: 0 1px 2px rgba(0, 0, 0, 0.5);
-moz-box-shadow: 0 1px 2px rgba(0, 0, 0, 0.5);
box-shadow: 0 1px 2px rgba(0, 0, 0, 0.5);
}
```

FIGURE 6.14 shows the results in Safari after adding a box-shadow to the button that's just 1px from the top with a 2px blur. For color, we're using black at 50% using RGBA, so that the shadow will have some transparency to it, letting the background behind it shine through.

And that not only completes our button, but our entire form as well. Using a few extra lines of CSS3, we've molded an otherwise default-looking form into something a bit more stylized and in line with the rest of the page design. We've chosen to use CSS3 here instead of images, as it's perfectly OK and harmless for browsers that don't yet support these advanced rules. Let's take a look to make sure.

WHAT ABOUT OTHER BROWSERS?

If we view our form in Internet Explorer 7, a browser that has zero support for CSS3, we see a perfectly acceptable, functional form (FIG 6.15). And that's great news! All the enhancements we added via a handful of CSS3 rules in the stylesheet have been safely ignored, leaving a bare-bones form that acts exactly as it should. Mission accomplished.

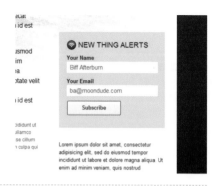

FIG 6.15: In IE7, the form looks like a normal form. And functions like one, too. This is good.

USING BOX-SHADOW TO CREATE FOCUS STATES

We could go a step further in our enrichment of this form's interactions by using the box-shadow property on the inputs' focus state. It's quick, easy, and like the aforementioned CSS3, degrades beautifully.

It requires simply creating a new declaration and adding the :focus pseudo-class to the attribute selector for text inputs.

(By the way, the preceding paragraph is a sure-fire pickup line, should you be in need of one. Thank me later.)

```
#thing-alerts input[type="text"]:focus {
    -webkit-box-shadow: 0 0 12px rgba(51, 204, 255, 0.5);
    -moz-box-shadow: 0 0 12px rgba(51, 204, 255, 0.5);
    box-shadow: 0 0 12px rgba(51, 204, 255, 0.5);
}
```

This declaration includes a box-shadow stack applying a bright blue shadow at 50% opacity around the text inputs when they are focused. We see the results in **FIGURE 6.16**, where we're mimicking the default OS behavior of focused inputs, but in creating our own we have much more control over the appearance.

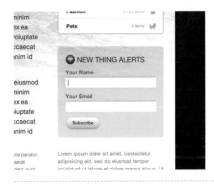

Browsers that don't support box-shadow? Well they just get a normal input when focused. And I'll bet you can guess what I'm about to say…yep, that's perfectly OK.

ADDING CSS ANIMATIONS TO ENRICH FORM INTERACTIONS

Going even a step further with the box-shadow on focus treatment, what if the shadow was *animated* as well, perhaps pulsing as if waiting for you to type. Let's briefly take a dip into the world of CSS Animations to make that happen.

Like CSS Transforms and Transitions, CSS Animations were initially developed by the WebKit team, then folded back into a proposed standard at the W3C (http://bkaprt.com/css3-2/20/). They work in Safari 4+, Chrome 4+, Firefox 5+, IE 10+, and Opera 15+ (curiously supporting the -webkit- vendor prefix). The support adoption has been a bit slower for Animations, and because of that I don't place as much attention on them (at least for now). And while they *are* powerful and exciting, it remains to be seen whether their adoption will be as comprehensive and swift as Transforms and Transitions have been, which already have decent (and growing) support.

Nonetheless, the concept and syntax for creating CSS Animations is rather straightforward, and for non-critical enhancements that only recent browsers will enjoy, it's fun to inject them into appropriate places. Let's add a simple animation to the focus state of the input to get a sense of how it all works.

Working with keyframes

The first part of building a CSS animation is to create a keyframes declaration. Those familiar with programming might relate this to building a function that can be called and referenced elsewhere in the stylesheet.

A keyframe is a specialized CSS at-rule. It's similar to a normal CSS declaration, but allows you to name it with an identifier and specify CSS rules and changes over the duration with a list of percentage values (or the keywords "to" and "from").

It'll make more sense to just see one in practice, so let's create a simple animation that will fade in and fade out the box-shadow we previously added to focused form inputs.

We'll name it "pulse" and set three rules that differ slightly: one at the starting point (0%), one at the halfway point (50%), and one at the end (100%). Each percentage rule is just adjusting the level of opacity of the blue box-shadow, from 20% up to 90% and back down to 20%. This change, transitioned over time and looped, will create the appearance of the input pulsing when focused in WebKit-powered browsers.

```
@ keyframes pulse {
  0% {
    box-shadow: 0 0 12px rgba(51, 204, 255, 0.2);
  }
  50% {
    box-shadow: 0 0 12px rgba(51, 204, 255, 0.9);
  }
  100% {
    box-shadow: 0 0 12px rgba(51, 204, 255, 0.2);
  }
}
```

Here I'm showing the non-vendor-prefixed version of the keyframe at-rule which recent versions of Firefox and IE will support. For Webkit and Opera browsers, we'll want to duplicate with the `-webkit-` prefix.

```
@-webkit-keyframes pulse {
  0% {
    box-shadow: 0 0 12px rgba(51, 204, 255, 0.2);
    }
  50% {
    box-shadow: 0 0 12px rgba(51, 204, 255, 0.9);
    }
  100% {
    box-shadow: 0 0 12px rgba(51, 204, 255, 0.2);
    }
  }

@keyframes pulse {
  0% {
    box-shadow: 0 0 12px rgba(51, 204, 255, 0.2);
    }
  50% {
    box-shadow: 0 0 12px rgba(51, 204, 255, 0.9);
    }
  100% {
    box-shadow: 0 0 12px rgba(51, 204, 255, 0.2);
    }
  }
```

Referencing the keyframe

The second part of a CSS animation is referencing the `keyframe` by name using the `animation` property.

In this case, we want this pulsing of the `box-shadow` to run when a user focuses a text input in the form. Here we'll call the `keyframe` by name, set a duration for the animation to run, loop it infinitely, and finally set the transition timing function of easing in and then easing out. You can see how the syntax for animation is similar to that of a transition.

```
#thing-alerts input[type="text"]:focus {
  -webkit-animation: pulse 1.5s infinite ease-in-out;
  animation: pulse 1.5s infinite ease-in-out;
}
```

With that, we're ensuring that the pulse animation runs only when the user focuses a text input on the form.

The result is quite stunning. And if technology enabled me to show you here on this piece of paper, I would. Instead, **FIGURE 6.17** will hopefully give you a sense of what happens: a slow, animated fade in/out of the box-shadow as if the input is waiting to be interacted with.

I used the shorthand animation property to set the values for calling the animation all in one rule. Alternatively, you can specify each value with its own property like so (again, using the -webkit- vendor prefix first, then the non-prefixed rules):

```
#thing-alerts input[type="text"]:focus {
  -webkit-animation-name: pulse;
  -webkit-animation-duration: 1.5s;
  -webkit-animation-iteration-count: infinite;
  -webkit-animation-timing-function: ease-in-out;
  animation-name: pulse;
  animation-duration: 1.5s;
  animation-iteration-count: infinite;
  animation-timing-function: ease-in-out;
}
```

Reusing the animation on button hover

One of the nice things about creating keyframes is that they can be reused throughout the stylesheet within multiple declarations. For example, we could apply that same "pulse" animation to the submit button when it's hovered or focused, adding a Wii-like, blue-pulsing glow.

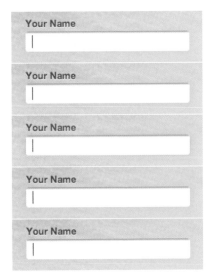

FIG 6.17: If you move your eyes up and down this image—quickly—you just might get a sense of the animation that we've added to the :focus state of the text inputs.

It's as simple as adding that same `animation` rule to a new `:hover/:focus` declaration for the submit button, just as we did with the text inputs:

```
#thing-alerts input[type="submit"]:hover,
#thing-alerts input[type="submit"]:focus {
   -webkit-animation: pulse 1.5s infinite ease-in-out;
   animation: pulse 1.5s infinite ease-in-out;
   }
```

The `pulse` animation we previously created for text inputs fades in and out a blue `box-shadow`—but we can use it here on the button as well, where the effect also works nicely (**FIG 6.18**), glowing softly when hovered or focused, as if waiting for the user to submit.

What about older browsers?

While they won't work in older browsers, CSS Animations are simple, require little overhead, and are safely ignored by

browsers that don't support them. What I've demonstrated
here with animations is rather rudimentary, barely scratching
the surface of what's possible on screen with just markup and
stylesheets. It's exciting stuff, and for that reason alone it's worth
experimenting with.

FOCUS ON INTERACTION

It's rare when form elements are also crucial brand elements,
and that's precisely why forms are a fantastic opportunity to
enhance with CSS3.

Form elements differ greatly in appearance depending on the
user's environment—but we can embrace those differences by
choosing to enrich them with advanced CSS, knowing things
will degrade to fully-functional, familiar, default form controls
in older browsers that don't support CSS3.

MICRO LAYOUTS

I MENTIONED at the beginning of the book that we're in need of a real layout solution with CSS. We've been bending the `float` property for over a decade to flexibly position content on the page, but lack a real system for laying out web pages. Which is kind of absurd when you think about it.

Fortunately there is much happening in CSS3 on the layout front. And in the spirit of the rest of this book, I'd like to share some CSS3 layout patterns that you can safely use today. Like the other examples in the book, if the browser doesn't support the styles we'll use, the user experience on your web page won't suffer. We'll focus on micro layouts rather than page structure—in other words, positioning individual components as opposed to columns and grids that make up entire pages.

By going through a few practical examples, you'll have a good grasp on the following CSS3 modules:

1. Multi-Column Layout
2. Flexible Box Layout (or flexbox)

These two new modules can help make previously-difficult layout problems for the CSS craftsperson a breeze—with no floats! And most importantly, we're going to use their awesome power in situations where the fallback is fine if the CSS3 properties are unsupported.

MULTI-COLUMN LAYOUT

Of all the new layout efforts happening in the world of CSS3, multi-column layout is by far the simplest to grasp and implement. Again, we won't be using it for structuring entire pages, but rather to enhance smaller chunks of a design.

The W3C explains the multi-column layout module (http://bkaprt.com/css3-2/21/):

> By using functionality described in this document, style sheets can declare that the content of an element is to be laid out in multiple columns.
>
> On the Web, tables have also been used to describe multi-column layouts. The main benefit of using CSS-based columns is flexibility; content can flow from one column to another, and the number of columns can vary depending on the size of the viewport. Removing presentation table markup from documents allows them to more easily be presented on various output devices including speech synthesizers and small mobile devices.

Well that sounds rather applicable to today's design requirements, doesn't it? Multi-column layout is especially good at flowing content into columns, while ensuring smooth fallback into a single column. Let's dive in to some simple examples to get a handle on how it works.

Let's say we have a `<div>` that contains multiple paragraphs in the Things We Left on the Moon example site. I'll add a class on the `<div>` that we'll apply the layout rules to:

```
<div class="multi">
    <p>Lorem ipsum dolor sit amet, consectetur adipisicing
       elit, sed do eiusmod tempor incididunt ut labore
```

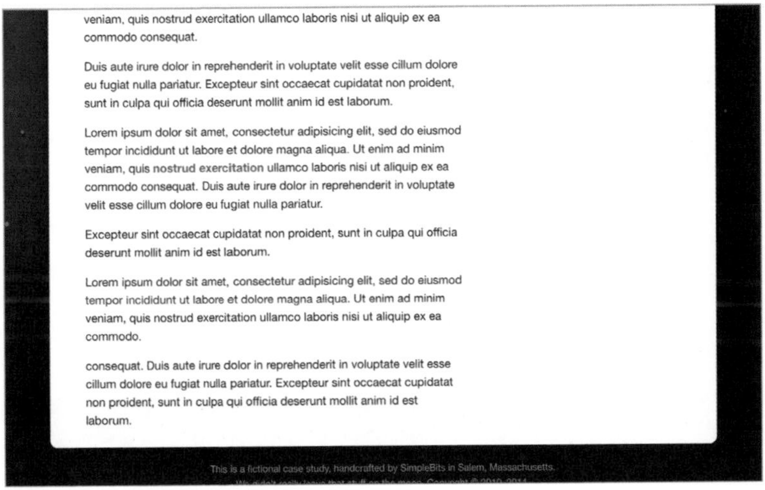

veniam, quis nostrud exercitation ullamco laboris nisi ut aliquip ex ea
commodo consequat.

Duis aute irure dolor in reprehenderit in voluptate velit esse cillum dolore
eu fugiat nulla pariatur. Excepteur sint occaecat cupidatat non proident,
sunt in culpa qui officia deserunt mollit anim id est laborum.

Lorem ipsum dolor sit amet, consectetur adipisicing elit, sed do eiusmod
tempor incididunt ut labore et dolore magna aliqua. Ut enim ad minim
veniam, quis nostrud exercitation ullamco laboris nisi ut aliquip ex ea
commodo consequat. Duis aute irure dolor in reprehenderit in voluptate
velit esse cillum dolore eu fugiat nulla pariatur.

Excepteur sint occaecat cupidatat non proident, sunt in culpa qui officia
deserunt mollit anim id est laborum.

Lorem ipsum dolor sit amet, consectetur adipisicing elit, sed do eiusmod
tempor incididunt ut labore et dolore magna aliqua. Ut enim ad minim
veniam, quis nostrud exercitation ullamco laboris nisi ut aliquip ex ea
commodo.

consequat. Duis aute irure dolor in reprehenderit in voluptate velit esse
cillum dolore eu fugiat nulla pariatur. Excepteur sint occaecat cupidatat
non proident, sunt in culpa qui officia deserunt mollit anim id est
laborum.

This is a fictional case study, handcrafted by SimpleBits in Salem, Massachusetts.

FIG 7.1: A block of unstyled paragraphs.

```
        et dolore magna aliqua. Ut enim ad minim veniam,
        quis nostrud exercitation ullamco laboris nisi ut
        aliquip ex ea commodo consequat.</p>
        <p>Duis aute irure dolor in …
    …
</div>
```

If we wished to lay out this particular group of paragraphs
into multiple columns (**FIG 7.1**), we could add a bit of progressive
enhancement here and apply a multi-column layout style that
does just that: the column-count property. (Notice I'm specifying
styles for Webkit and Mozilla browsers as well as an unprefixed
property here.)

```
div.multi {
    -webkit-column-count: 3;
    -moz-column-count: 3;
    column-count: 3;
}
```

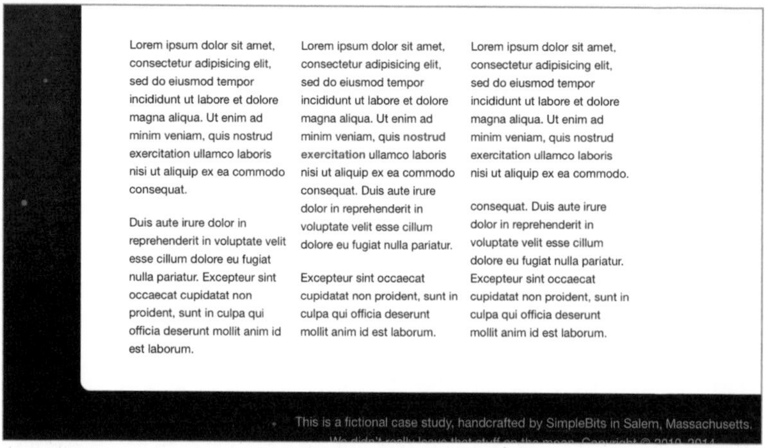

Lorem ipsum dolor sit amet, consectetur adipisicing elit, sed do eiusmod tempor incididunt ut labore et dolore magna aliqua. Ut enim ad minim veniam, quis nostrud exercitation ullamco laboris nisi ut aliquip ex ea commodo consequat.

Duis aute irure dolor in reprehenderit in voluptate velit esse cillum dolore eu fugiat nulla pariatur. Excepteur sint occaecat cupidatat non proident, sunt in culpa qui officia deserunt mollit anim id est laborum.

Lorem ipsum dolor sit amet, consectetur adipisicing elit, sed do eiusmod tempor incididunt ut labore et dolore magna aliqua. Ut enim ad minim veniam, quis nostrud exercitation ullamco laboris nisi ut aliquip ex ea commodo consequat. Duis aute irure dolor in reprehenderit in voluptate velit esse cillum dolore eu fugiat nulla pariatur.

Excepteur sint occaecat cupidatat non proident, sunt in culpa qui officia deserunt mollit anim id est laborum.

Lorem ipsum dolor sit amet, consectetur adipisicing elit, sed do eiusmod tempor incididunt ut labore et dolore magna aliqua. Ut enim ad minim veniam, quis nostrud exercitation ullamco laboris nisi ut aliquip ex ea commodo.

consequat. Duis aute irure dolor in reprehenderit in voluptate velit esse cillum dolore eu fugiat nulla pariatur. Excepteur sint occaecat cupidatat non proident, sunt in culpa qui officia deserunt mollit anim id est laborum.

This is a fictional case study, handcrafted by SimpleBits in Salem, Massachusetts.

FIG 7.2: Three columns created by using the `column-count` property.

FIGURE 7.2 shows the result: the paragraphs flow equally into three columns, resembling a newspaper article.

Pretty magical, and no floats! Additionally, we can specify a gutter between the columns using the `column-gap` property.

```
div.multi {
  -webkit-column-count: 3;
  -webkit-column-gap: 30px;
  -moz-column-count: 3;
  -moz-column-gap: 30px;
  column-count: 3;
  column-gap: 30px;
}
```

FIGURE 7.3 shows the 30px gap in between columns—but only between them and not on the outside of the grouping. When I saw this implemented I did a little dance, for as you also probably know, assigning margins between floated columns but not the last column is always somewhat of a pain. This should be easy! And multi-column layout makes it so.

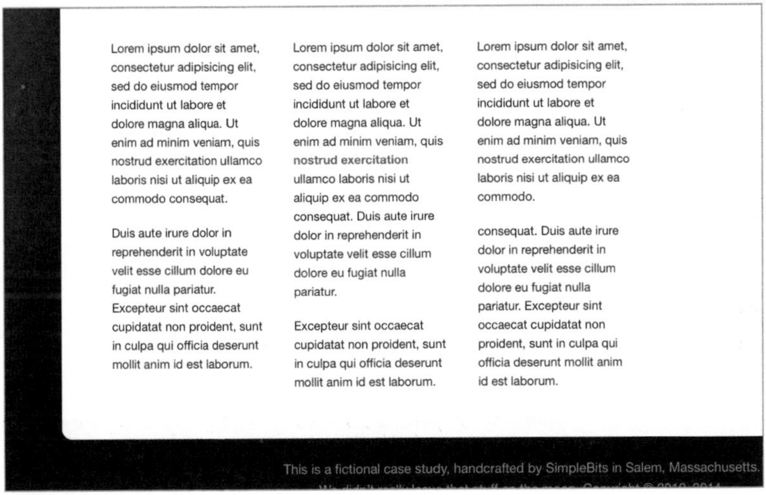

Lorem ipsum dolor sit amet, consectetur adipisicing elit, sed do eiusmod tempor incididunt ut labore et dolore magna aliqua. Ut enim ad minim veniam, quis nostrud exercitation ullamco laboris nisi ut aliquip ex ea commodo consequat.

Duis aute irure dolor in reprehenderit in voluptate velit esse cillum dolore eu fugiat nulla pariatur. Excepteur sint occaecat cupidatat non proident, sunt in culpa qui officia deserunt mollit anim id est laborum.

Lorem ipsum dolor sit amet, consectetur adipisicing elit, sed do eiusmod tempor incididunt ut labore et dolore magna aliqua. Ut enim ad minim veniam, quis nostrud exercitation ullamco laboris nisi ut aliquip ex ea commodo consequat. Duis aute irure dolor in reprehenderit in voluptate velit esse cillum dolore eu fugiat nulla pariatur.

Excepteur sint occaecat cupidatat non proident, sunt in culpa qui officia deserunt mollit anim id est laborum.

Lorem ipsum dolor sit amet, consectetur adipisicing elit, sed do eiusmod tempor incididunt ut labore et dolore magna aliqua. Ut enim ad minim veniam, quis nostrud exercitation ullamco laboris nisi ut aliquip ex ea commodo.

consequat. Duis aute irure dolor in reprehenderit in voluptate velit esse cillum dolore eu fugiat nulla pariatur. Excepteur sint occaecat cupidatat non proident, sunt in culpa qui officia deserunt mollit anim id est laborum.

This is a fictional case study, handcrafted by SimpleBits in Salem, Massachusetts.

FIG 7.3: Adding gutters between the columns with `column-gap`.

Another feature of multi-column layout is the option of having a border separator between the columns. Let's add a one-pixel, grey line between each column using the `column-rule` property, which takes values just like `border` does.

```
div.multi {
    -webkit-column-count: 3;
    -webkit-column-gap: 30px;
    -webkit-column-rule: 1px solid #ddd;
    -moz-column-count: 3;
    -moz-column-gap: 30px;
    -moz-column-rule: 1px solid #ddd;
    column-count: 3;
    column-gap: 30px;
    column-rule: 1px solid #ddd;
}
```

Presto! Equal-height borders that magically appear in the center of the column gutters (**FIG 7.4**). All with a few simple CSS3 declarations.

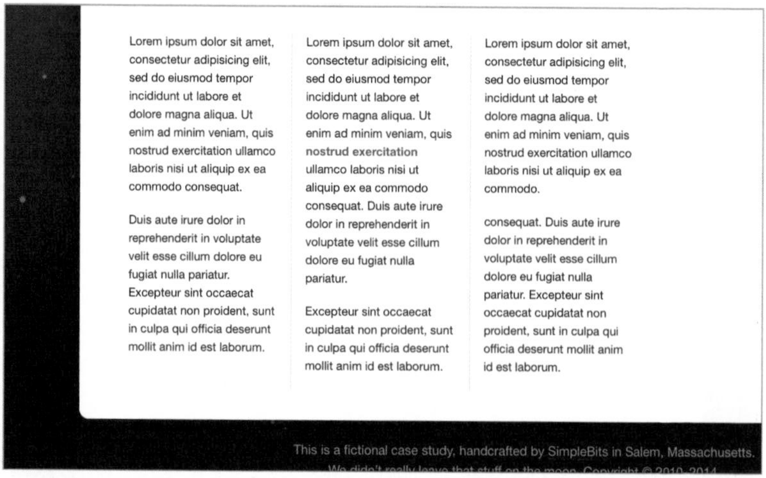

This is a fictional case study, handcrafted by SimpleBits in Salem, Massachusetts.
We didn't really leave that stuff on the moon. Copyright © 2010–2014

FIG 7.4: Equal-height borders between columns using `column-rule`.

Spanning multiple columns

Now let's say we had an element within `<div class="multi">` that we wanted to span across all the columns, instead of flowing into one of them. For example, if we added a heading above the group of paragraphs.

```
<div class="multi">
  <h4>This spans the columns</h4>
  <p>Lorem ipsum …
  …
</div>
```

FIGURE 7.5 shows how the heading will be part of the first column, with the paragraphs flowing in after it, which isn't what we want to have happen.

If we apply the `column-span` property with a value of `all`, the heading will work as we'd like it to (**FIG 7.6**).

This spans the columns	Lorem ipsum dolor sit amet,	consectetur adipisicing elit,
Lorem ipsum dolor sit amet, consectetur adipisicing elit, sed do eiusmod tempor incididunt ut labore et dolore magna aliqua. Ut enim ad minim veniam, quis	consectetur adipisicing elit, sed do eiusmod tempor incididunt ut labore et dolore magna aliqua. Ut enim ad minim veniam, quis nostrud exercitation ullamco laboris nisi ut	sed do eiusmod tempor incididunt ut labore et dolore magna aliqua. Ut enim ad minim veniam, quis nostrud exercitation ullamco laboris nisi ut aliquip ex ea commodo.

FIG 7.5: Adding a heading makes the paragraphs flow through the three columns.

This spans the columns via the column-span property

Lorem ipsum dolor sit amet,	Lorem ipsum dolor sit amet,	Lorem ipsum dolor sit amet,
consectetur adipisicing elit, sed do eiusmod tempor incididunt ut labore et dolore magna aliqua. Ut enim ad minim veniam, quis nostrud exercitation ullamco	consectetur adipisicing elit, sed do eiusmod tempor incididunt ut labore et dolore magna aliqua. Ut enim ad minim veniam, quis nostrud exercitation	consectetur adipisicing elit, sed do eiusmod tempor incididunt ut labore et dolore magna aliqua. Ut enim ad minim veniam, quis nostrud exercitation ullamco

FIG 7.6: Use column-span to make an element defy the columns and span the full width.

```
div.multi h4 {
  -webkit-column-span: all;
  -moz-column-span: all;
  column-span: all;
}
```

The spanning will work regardless of where the element falls in the markup. **FIGURE 7.7** shows the header breaking through the columns in the middle of the grouping of paragraphs.

What about browser support?

Multi-Column Layout is a W3C Candidate Recommendation and works in Safari 3+, Chrome 3+, Firefox 2+, Opera 11.1+, and IE 10+. Pretty excellent coverage in recent browsers—but again, since the fallback is just one column of text in this case, it's a rather safe enhancement to make. If columns are crucial to

Lorem ipsum dolor sit amet, consectetur adipisicing elit, sed do eiusmod tempor incididunt ut labore et dolore magna aliqua. Ut enim ad minim veniam, quis nostrud exercitation ullamco laboris nisi ut aliquip ex ea commodo consequat.

Duis aute irure dolor in

reprehenderit in voluptate velit esse cillum dolore eu fugiat nulla pariatur. Excepteur sint occaecat cupidatat non proident, sunt in culpa qui officia deserunt mollit anim id est laborum.

Lorem ipsum dolor sit amet, consectetur adipisicing elit, sed do eiusmod tempor

incididunt ut labore et dolore magna aliqua. Ut enim ad minim veniam, quis nostrud exercitation ullamco laboris nisi ut aliquip ex ea commodo consequat. Duis aute irure dolor in reprehenderit in voluptate velit esse cillum dolore eu fugiat nulla pariatur.

This spans the columns via the column-span property

Excepteur sint occaecat cupidatat non proident, sunt in culpa qui officia deserunt mollit anim id est laborum.

Lorem ipsum dolor sit amet, consectetur adipisicing elit, sed do eiusmod tempor

incididunt ut labore et dolore magna aliqua. Ut enim ad minim veniam, quis nostrud exercitation ullamco laboris nisi ut aliquip ex ea commodo.

consequat. Duis aute irure

dolor in reprehenderit in voluptate velit esse cillum dolore eu fugiat nulla pariatur. Excepteur sint occaecat cupidatat non proident, sunt in culpa qui officia deserunt mollit anim id est laborum.

This is a fictional case study, handcrafted by SimpleBits in Salem, Massachusetts.

FIG 7.7: column-span will even work in within the multi-column layout.

the design and/or message the site is conveying, then you might opt for another solution.

For micro layouts that happen within larger page structures, multi-column layout is pretty darn handy and simple to fold in. Just be aware that using it for large amounts of text could force the reader to scroll up and down the multiple columns in order to read, which isn't ideal. For micro layout patterns, however, multi-column layout is quite useful. Let's look at another quick easy win in regards to forms.

Column-izing form elements

Here's a simple example of using multi-column layout in a situation where it's perfectly okay if the browser doesn't support it. If we added a group of checkboxes to the "New Thing Alerts Form" on our case study site, we might mark them up in an unordered list like so:

FIG 7.8: The Thing Alerts form with checkbox options added.

```
<fieldset>
  <h4>Interested in...</h4>
  <ul class="options">
    <li>
      <label><input type="checkbox" /> Junk</label>
    </li>
    <li>
      <label><input type="checkbox" /> Conspiracies »
        </label>
    </li>
    ...
  </ul>
</fieldset>
```

FIGURE 7.8 shows how that list of seven checkbox options might look on the page.

Notice all the wasted space to the right of those short, one-word labels. This is a perfect pattern for applying a multi-column

FIG 7.9: Multi-column layout is perfect for organizing form elements to maximize available space.

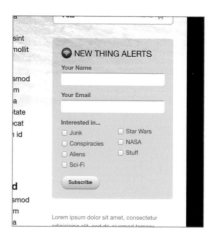

layout for browsers that support it. One long list is perfectly fine, but for efficiency, let's make these items flow into two columns, with a 10px gutter between.

```
ul.options {
    -webkit-column-count: 2;
    -webkit-column-gap: 20px;
    -moz-column-count: 2;
    -moz-column-gap: 20px;
    column-count: 2;
    column-gap: 20px;
}
```

FIGURE 7.9 shows the checkbox list putting each `<li>` into two columns, making better use of the space.

Again, this micro layout works perfectly fine as one column, but is enhanced and more efficient with two, should the browser support multi-column layout. Fortunately, most recent browsers do support it, so be on the lookout for situations where multiple columns may make your designs smarter.

FLEXBOXING THE FUTURE

I'm going to end this chapter (and the book in general) with a glimpse into the future. While the Flexible Box Layout Module—more commonly referred to as flexbox—is still a Working Draft at the W3C, it has gained a lot of momentum and can be a viable option for solving micro layout challenges. Recent browsers have introduced support for flexbox, and it clearly makes some of the impossible possible when it comes to CSS layout puzzles. It's an exciting time, folks.

It's important to note that flexbox is designed specifically for micro layouts (small modules within the page), while the forthcoming Grid Layout (http://bkaprt.com/css3-2/22/) will be meant for entire page layouts. (See Jake Archibald's convincing argument for not using flexbox for page layout, where he describes how it can lead to unfortunate, shaky initial loading of the page: http://bkaprt.com/css3-2/23/.)

I'll be barely scratching the surface here in terms of what flexbox can accomplish, but a few practical examples of how it can be used within a larger layout system should help you get off to the races.

So, just what is the Flexible Box Layout Module? Here's what the W3C says about it (http://bkaprt.com/css3-2/24/):

In the flex layout model, the children of a flex container can be laid out in any direction, and can "flex" their sizes, either growing to fill unused space or shrinking to avoid overflowing the parent. Both horizontal and vertical alignment of the children can be easily manipulated.

Well hey, that actually makes sense... and it's exciting! Horizontal and vertical alignment can be manipulated?! Like using <table>s for layout, but with semantic markup? This is the magic wand we've been waiting for, folks. The future is bright.

Flexbox is very powerful and far more complex than, say, Multi-Column Layout. Reading the spec throws a visual person such as myself into a state of confusion, but seeing examples in

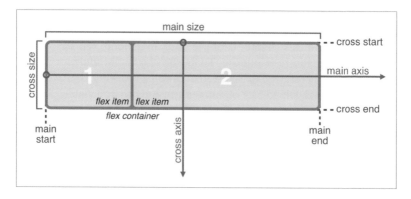

FIG 7.10: The W3C's explanation of the flexbox box model and how it names the various directions and sizing terms used to define how a container can apply flex to its children. Don't worry about these terms just yet. (http://bkaprt.com/css3-2/26/)

action makes it all palatable. So, we'll be going through a few examples in this chapter to give you a primer on using flexbox in a few practical situations, and ones where the layout is non-critical and can fall back to something acceptable.

I can't recommend Chris Coyier's A Complete Guide to Flexbox enough (http://bkaprt.com/css3-2/25/). Chris has created the most comprehensive, yet easily understandable reference on using flexbox that I've found, which he describes as such:

> The main idea behind the flex layout is to give the container the ability to alter its items' width/height (and order) to best fill the available space (mostly to accommodate to all kind of display devices and screen sizes). A flex container expands items to fill available free space, or shrinks them to prevent overflow.

This expanding and shrinking of elements within a flex container can happen across multiple axes, as shown in the arguably decipherable diagram from the W3C in FIGURE 7.10.

So, the first thing to grasp here is that in order to implement flexbox, we'll need a container to declare its contents as flexible items. And there are CSS properties that pertain to both the container and the items within it.

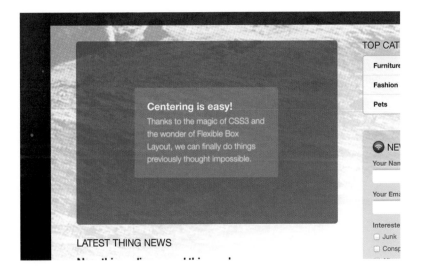

FIG 7.11: Behold! Vertical centering with CSS!

Vertical centering

Baffling front-end devs for over a decade, the lack of a true vertical centering mechanism in CSS has been an almost laughable omission. I recall several times trying to explain to non-designers that, "no, there's really no reliable way to do that." A blank stare of disbelief usually follows. Then, "well just use a `<table>`."

Fortunately, flexbox finally solves this! Let's go through an extremely simple example to demonstrate. **FIGURE 7.11** shows a lovely purple container, with a box of content that's centered both horizontally and vertically.

The markup for this little pattern could look something like this:

```
<div class="container">
  <div>
    <h5>Centering is easy!</h5>
    <p>Thanks to the magic of CSS3 and the wonder … </p>
  </div>
</div>
```

It's essentially a container wrapped around a block of heading and paragraph. Simple stuff.

Now let's add the flexbox magic here to get things centered. In this case, all of our flexbox properties will get applied on the container. I'm going to show the example using only the essential, non-prefixed properties and values for now, and we'll loop back around to browser compatibility later.

```
div.container {
  height: 300px;
  display: flex;
  align-items: center;
  justify-content: center;
}
```

So we have a box that's 300px tall, and we want to the items within to be centered vertically and horizontally. The first rule we need on this container is display: flex; which tells the browser the contents of this element will be flexible. This enables flexbox on this particular container.

Secondly, align-items is a flexbox property that tells the browser how to align the contents of the container along the cross axis (vertical). We've set that to center here, but other values include flex-start, flex-end, stretch, and baseline. If we'd said align-items: flex-end;, for example, the items in the container would stick to the bottom of the box (FIG 7.12).

Lastly, justify-content: center; ensures the items in the container are centered horizontally.

And folks, that's it for perfect centering in CSS3 using flexbox. Should the contents or dimensions of the box change, flexbox will keep it centered no matter what (FIG 7.13). As you can imagine, this is especially handy when dealing with flexible layouts on various device screen sizes.

Vendor prefixing flexbox

Using flexbox does require vendor prefixes, like most of the other examples in this book. Because the specification evolved

FIG 7.12: Using the `flex-end` value will stick items to the bottom of the container.

FIG 7.13: Flexbox centering is ideal for adapting to various viewport widths.

over time, the prefixes are a bit more verbose in order to support the widest possible set of browsers, but only slightly more cumbersome than other CSS3 properties.

Let's properly fill out our vertical centering example with all the necessary vendor-prefixed properties. The comments next to each line should give you a clear picture of why they're necessary.

```
div.container {
  height: 300px;
  display: -webkit-box;    /* Old Safari, iOS, Android */
  display: -moz-box;       /* Old firefox */
  display: -ms-flexbox;    /* IE 10 */
  display: -webkit-flex;   /* Chrome 21-28, Safari 6.1+ */
  display: flex;           /* IE 11, Chrome 29+,
                              Opera 12.1+, Firefox 22+ */
  align-items: center;
  justify-content: center;
}
```

Older versions of Webkit and Mozilla started using the `-box` value to trigger flexbox, while IE 10 started using `-flexbox`. Eventually, `-flex` was settled on as a standard. Because of this evolution, our stack gets a little tall, but this will ensure support over older, newer, and future browsers.

We'll need to jump through similar hoops for the `align-items` and `justify-content` properties:

```
div.container {
  height: 300px;
  display: -webkit-box;    /* Old Safari, iOS, Android */
  display: -moz-box;       /* Old firefox */
  display: -ms-flexbox;    /* IE 10 */
  display: -webkit-flex;   /* Chrome 21-28, Safari 6.1+ */
  display: flex;           /* IE 11, Chrome 29+,
                              Opera 12.1+, Firefox 22+ */
```

```
    align-items: center;
    justify-content: center;
    -webkit-box-align: center;
    -moz-box-align: center;
    -ms-flex-align: center;
    -webkit-align-items: center;
    align-items: center;

    -webkit-box-pack: center;
    -moz-box-pack: center;
    -ms-flex-pack: center;
    -webkit-justify-content: center;
    justify-content: center;
}
```

As I've said earlier in the book, don't be scared off by vendor prefixes! There's a method to the madness, and it's always worth the trouble. For more on flexbox properties and their corresponding prefixes, check out "Designing CSS Layouts With Flexbox Is As Easy As Pie" (http://bkaprt.com/css3-2/27/) by David Storey.

Note: For the next two flexbox examples, I'm going to refrain from showing the vendor prefixes so that it's easier to grasp what's happening. Just keep in mind you'll need to add them in order to support more browsers.

Bulletproofing a search row

Here's a simple example of how flexbox can aid in bulletproofing the widths of certain elements. **FIGURE 7.14** shows a fairly common horizontal search input and button pattern. Notice how we have two variable width items ("Search" text and "Go" button) while the text input field fills out the rest of the remaining space. Without setting a specific fixed width on all the items, this is a difficult task. Flexbox makes this easy—and not only that, but also flexible—regardless of the text on either side or viewport width. Truly bulletproof.

FIG 7.14: A flexible search row that maximizes its horizontal space using flexbox.

FIG 7.15: Without flexbox, the form may not take advantage of all the available space.

The markup for the form is elementary here:

```
<form class="search">
  <label>Search</label>
  <input type="text" />
  <input type="submit" value="Go" />
</form>
```

I'm omitting the purely decorative styles attached here (and having read the previous chapters of the book, you'll know how to do this anyway!). But without flexbox applied, we get a bit of a ragged string of elements, with the text input taking up an arbitrary amount of space (**FIG 7.15**).

Not exactly optimal, and the vertical alignment of the items is also a bit out of whack. Let's flex some muscle.

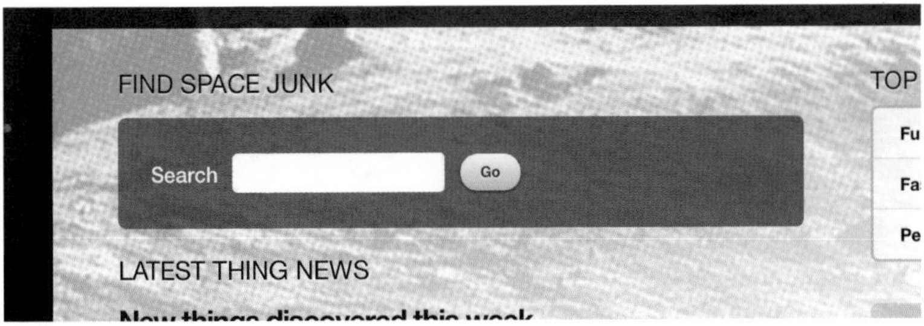

FIG 7.16: Flexbox is already helping tighten up the vertical alignment.

First step is to "activate flex mode" (yes, my kids have been watching *Power Rangers*) on the form. While we're at it, we'll also set alignment of the items to center.

```
form.search {
  display: flex;
  align-items: center;
  }
```

Things are looking tighter in terms of vertical alignment (**FIG 7.16**). Hooray! Next, let's use the flex-grow property on the text input to fill out any remaining space in the box.

```
form.search input[type="text"] {
  flex-grow: 1;
  }
```

By setting flex-grow with a value of 1, we're telling it to take up as much space that's available within the flex container (in this case, the form).

I like Chris Coyier's lucid definition of the flex-grow property (http://bkaprt.com/css3-2/25/):

This defines the ability for a flex item to grow if necessary. It accepts a unitless value that serves as a proportion. It dictates what amount of the available space inside the flex container the item should take up.

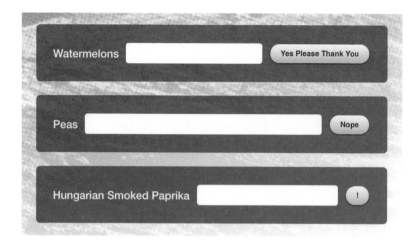

FIG 7.17: Flexbox makes bulletproof, full-width, form rows a snap to create.

> *If all items have* `flex-grow` *set to 1, every child will set to an equal size inside the container. If you were to give one of the children a value of 2, that child would take up twice as much space as the others.*

So, since the text input is the only item we're assigning `flex-grow` to, it will automatically fill in the remaining space available. If we changed the label and button text, the input would adjust as needed (**FIG 7.17**).

Without flexbox here, we'd need to set pixel-based widths on everything, making a very rigid, inflexible system. With flexbox, we're getting the visual layout we want, with the added flexibility of not relying on the content. As you can imagine, the flex here makes it also perfect for fluid layouts and/or those that can adapt to varying screen widths.

I like this example a lot because it's a small, simple way you can start using flexbox that degrades nicely. If the older browser doesn't support it, then the form is still functional and readable. It just doesn't stretch to the grid. And that's OK.

This is a slat

Lorem ipsum dolor sit amet, consectetur adipisicing elit, sed do eiusmod tempor incididunt ut labore et dolore magna aliqua. Ut enim ad minim veniam, quis nostrud exercitation ullamco laboris nisi ut aliquip ex ea commodo consequat.

Duis aute irure dolor in reprehenderit in voluptate velit esse cillum dolore eu fugiat nulla pariatur. Excepteur sint occaecat cupidatat non proident, sunt in culpa qui officia deserunt mollit anim id est laborum.

FIG 7.18: An example of the ubiquitous "slat" module.

Flexing with "slats"

For the final example of the book, I'm going to share how flexbox makes it so much simpler to deal with slats. I call them slats, some call them media objects or modules. Regardless, it's a common pattern of an avatar, image, or icon on the left, and text on the right, with each taking up a column.

FIGURE 7.18 shows a simple example within our case study site. We'd typically use `float` and specific widths and/or margins to achieve that, and while that works, flexbox can make this far easier and, like the previous search bar example, bulletproof and flexible in a variety of environments.

The markup for our slat example might look something like the following:

This is a slat

Lorem ipsum dolor sit amet, consectetur adipisicing elit, sed
do eiusmod tempor incididunt ut labore et dolore magna
aliqua. Ut enim ad minim veniam, quis nostrud exercitation
ullamco laboris nisi ut aliquip ex ea commodo consequat.

Duis aute irure dolor in reprehenderit in voluptate velit esse
cillum dolore eu fugiat nulla pariatur. Excepteur sint occaecat
cupidatat non proident, sunt in culpa qui officia deserunt mollit
anim id est laborum.

FIG 7.19: The image is stretching to match the height of the copy, which isn't what we want.

```
<div class="slat">
    <img src="rover.jpg" width="200" class="slat-image" />
    <div class="slat-copy">
        <h5>This is a slat</h5>
        <p>Lorem ipsum dolor sit amet, consectetur …</p>
        …
    </div>
</div>
```

A container with an image, and another container for the text
content. Notice I'm setting a width of 200px on the slat image.
We'll be adjusting that later to show the flexbox magic in action.
First, let's activate flex mode on the slat container:

```
div.slat {
    display: flex;
}
```

FIGURE 7.19 shows the results; the items appear side by
side, but the image stretches to match the height of the content. That's due to the default behavior of items within a flex

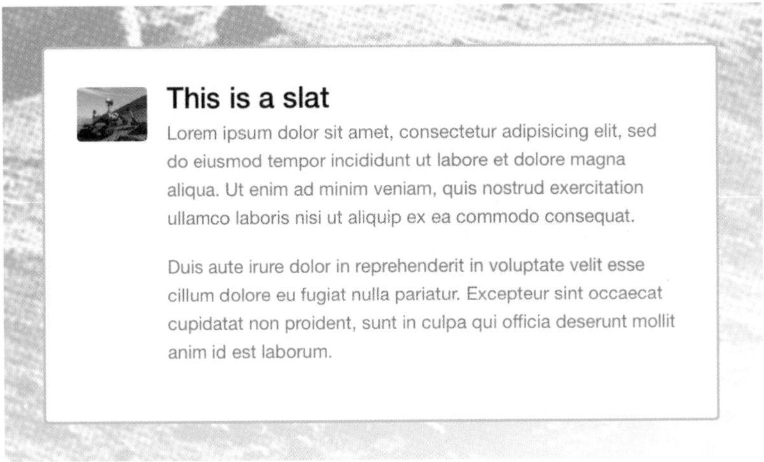

This is a slat

Lorem ipsum dolor sit amet, consectetur adipisicing elit, sed do eiusmod tempor incididunt ut labore et dolore magna aliqua. Ut enim ad minim veniam, quis nostrud exercitation ullamco laboris nisi ut aliquip ex ea commodo consequat.

Duis aute irure dolor in reprehenderit in voluptate velit esse cillum dolore eu fugiat nulla pariatur. Excepteur sint occaecat cupidatat non proident, sunt in culpa qui officia deserunt mollit anim id est laborum.

FIG 7.20: Getting closer, but the image width still needs work.

container—they'll stretch across the cross axis to fill out available space. Let's fix that by using the `flex-start` value on `align-items`, which will override that default.

```
div.slat {
  display: flex;
  align-items: flex-start;
}
```

FIGURE 7.20 shows things looking a bit better, although the image width of 200px isn't being reflected. Let's fix that by adding the `flex` property to `div.slat-copy` container.

```
div.slat {
  display: flex;
  align-items: flex-start;
}

div.slat div.slat-copy {
  flex: 1;
}
```

This is a slat

Lorem ipsum dolor sit amet, consectetur adipisicing elit, sed do eiusmod tempor incididunt ut labore et dolore magna aliqua. Ut enim ad minim veniam, quis nostrud exercitation ullamco laboris nisi ut aliquip ex ea commodo consequat.

Duis aute irure dolor in reprehenderit in voluptate velit esse cillum dolore eu fugiat nulla pariatur. Excepteur sint occaecat cupidatat non proident, sunt in culpa qui officia deserunt mollit anim id est laborum.

FIG 7.21: Flexbox makes it simple to create slat layouts regardless of the media's width.

FIG 7.22: Swap in a different size image, and the layout automatically adjusts. Bulletproof!

The `flex` property is shorthand for the `flex-grow`, `flex-shrink` and `flex-basis` properties. What we're saying when assigning a single value here is to set `flex-grow` and `flex-shrink` to 1, and set `flex-basis` (the initial width of the item before shrinking or growing) to 0. **FIGURE 7.21** shows the intended slat layout with those simple flexbox rules and no floats. Again, the advantage here is that should the image of the left change in width, the text column will adjust its width accordingly (**FIG 7.22**).

THE FUTURE, NOW

As I mentioned earlier in the chapter, the goal here was to give you a glimpse into the future of layout, but with a few examples that you can sink your teeth into today. Look for patterns where flexbox could make your life easier, but that won't fall apart should the browser not support it. In the slat example, if the image and text are in one column rather than two, things are still readable and functional. And that's the most important part.

I hope that this primer gets you excited to experiment with flexbox and gets you ready for the future, which appears to be a simpler, more flexible place.

For more on flexbox, I highly recommend Zoe Gillenwater's presentation on the subject, which is filled with great practical examples (http://bkaprt.com/css3-2/28/) as well as Phillip Walton's collection of flexbox solutions to common design patterns (http://bkaprt.com/css3-2/29/).

CONCLUSION

Okay, let's come back down to earth now and decompress. We've covered a lot of wonderful (if I may say so) ways to use CSS3 right now in your daily work. My hope is that by demonstrating how these techniques can enhance the experience layer in browsers that support them, while gracefully degrading in browsers that don't, you'll be inspired to use them every day, regardless of the project you're working on.

The real promise of CSS3 is that it enables us to solve common design problems more efficiently, with less code and more flexibility. So long as you (and your clients and bosses) can accept that websites may look and be experienced differently in the browsers and devices that access them, then the sky's the limit. Jump right in.

I mentioned back in Chapter 1 that I often hear, "I can't wait to use CSS3—*when it's supported in all browsers.*" My goal with this book was to prove that you don't need to wait. Start experimenting with this stuff now. Begin using CSS3 for non-critical visual events in your designs. Now that you're armed with what works, and—more importantly—how things degrade when they don't, you can comfortably achieve what previously took more time and code, with only a few lines of CSS.

What about clients and bosses who don't get it?

Another question I often get asked when talking about CSS3 is how to use it in client work. How do you educate clients on the benefits of using CSS3 over other solutions? It's the education that's most helpful. Show your clients how much less code and how many fewer images there are. Show them how the experience differs in browsers that don't support CSS3. Explain the tradeoffs to them.

If that sounds like too much work, then *just do it.*

Start adding CSS3 to your daily work and let your clients and bosses happily discover it. The truth is, many of the examples I've demonstrated in this book are discoverable while experiencing the site: hovering, focusing, interacting, etc. That's intentional, of course.

Often, with my own client work, I'll add this experience enhancement into the project without saying a word about it, surprising and delighting the client when they stumble on it. And more importantly, surprising and delighting the client's *visitors* when *they* stumble upon it.

Getting this to work in every browser imaginable? Well, that will cost extra. Ahem.

Looking ahead

What about the future? The whole of CSS3 encompasses much, much more than can be covered in this small book. I wanted to focus very squarely on what's practically usable today, avoiding what's still being hashed out in other modules that perhaps don't have such widespread implementation.

But the track is a positive one. New property support is being added in almost every new iteration of WebKit, Mozilla, Opera, and Internet Explorer. This rapid adoption via vendor prefixing is what's driving innovation. Keeping tabs on what's new, and watching for a tipping point in implementation among these forward-thinking browsers, is what can educate you on real-world use.

Eventually, we'll be able to rely on CSS3 not only for experience enhancement, but for those critical visual concepts as well (page layout being a primary example). It's been a seemingly slow path to get there, but that's necessary for things to unfold correctly. While on that slow path, don't hesitate to grab hold and use what works in the present. You, your clients, and the web's citizens will benefit.

FURTHER READING AND RESOURCES

- CSS3.info has long been rounding up news, examples, and developments: http://www.CSS3.info
- Also see their preview section for demos of specific properties: http://www.CSS3.info/preview
- Earlier, I told you not to read the specs; but for a relevant big picture view, to prepare for what's ahead, and to see which modules are in what state (Working Draft, Candidate Recommendation, etc.), look here: http://www.w3.org/Style/CSS/current-work
- Or, go here for more on the modules themselves, how they're broken up, and what they contain: http://www.w3.org/TR/CSS3-roadmap

The development blogs for all the major browsers are a fantastic place to keep up on what's being implemented and when. I highly recommend subscribing to keep abreast of what's being adopted, rejected, and experimented with:

- http://webkit.org/blog
- http://blog.mozilla.com
- http://dev.opera.com/articles/css
- http://blogs.msdn.com/b/ie

Several sites have emerged to help understand browser compatibility and identify which versions support which properties:

- http://caniuse.com
- http://www.quirksmode.org/css/contents.html
- http://html5readiness.com *Don't let the URL fool you, as it contains CSS3 info as well.*

A number of browser-based tools provide a visual environment for creating the currently supported syntax, and serve as great learning tools:

- http://CSS3generator.com
- http://CSS3please.com
- http://gradients.glrzad.com
- http://tools.westciv.com
- http://border-radius.com

And finally, JavaScript solutions can assist in broadening the support for CSS3 to many additional browsers. For critical visual events that need to work everywhere using today's CSS3, there are options:

- http://www.modernizr.com
- http://ecsstender.org
- http://selectivizr.com/ *A pseudo-class selector emulation for IE5.5-8.*

Thanks for reading! Now go build wonderful things. Dream big and implement small.

REFERENCES

Shortened URLs are numbered sequentially; the related long URLs are listed below for reference.

Chapter 1

1 http://alistapart.com/article/tohell
2 http://www.w3.org/TR/css3-roadmap/#whymods
3 http://alistapart.com/article/prefix-or-posthack
4 http://www.chromium.org/blink#vendor-prefixes

Chapter 2

5 http://www.w3.org/TR/css3-transitions/
6 http://www.opera.com/docs/specs/presto23/css/transitions/
7 https://developer.mozilla.org/en-US/docs/Web/Guide/CSS/Using_CSS_transitions
8 http://www.w3.org/TR/css3-transitions/#properties-from-css-
9 http://trentwalton.com/2010/03/22/CSS3-in-transition/

Chapter 4

10 http://www.w3.org/TR/css-transforms-1/
11 http://www.w3.org/TR/css3-transforms/#transform-origin

Chapter 5

12 http://www.w3.org/TR/css3-background/
13 http://en.wikipedia.org/wiki/Parallax_scrolling
14 http://blog.teamtreehouse.com/how-to-recreate-silverbacks-parallax-effect
15 http://www.456bereastreet.com/archive/200601/css_3_selectors_explained/
16 http://www.quirksmode.org/css/contents.html
17 http://msdn.microsoft.com/en-us/library/cc351024%28VS.85%29.aspx

Chapter 6

18 http://www.westciv.com/tools/gradients/index-moz.html
19 http://snook.ca/archives/html_and_css/multiple-bg-css-gradients
20 http://www.w3.org/TR/css3-animations/

Chapter 7

21 http://www.w3.org/TR/css3-multicol
22 http://dev.w3.org/csswg/css-grid/
23 http://jakearchibald.com/2014/dont-use-flexbox-for-page-layout/
24 http://www.w3.org/TR/css-flexbox-1/
25 http://css-tricks.com/snippets/css/a-guide-to-flexbox/
26 http://www.w3.org/TR/css3-flexbox/#box-model
27 http://www.smashingmagazine.com/2013/05/22/centering-elements-with-flexbox/
28 http://zomigi.com/blog/leveling-up-with-flexbox/
29 http://philipwalton.github.io/solved-by-flexbox/

INDEX

ABOUT A BOOK APART

We cover the emerging and essential topics in web design and development with style, clarity, and above all, brevity—because working designer-developers can't afford to waste time.

COLOPHON

The text is set in FF Yoga and its companion, FF Yoga Sans, both by Xavier Dupré. Headlines and cover are set in Titling Gothic by David Berlow.

MIX
Paper from
responsible sources
FSC® C103203

This book was printed in the United States using FSC certified Finch papers.